NAVIGATING THE RACE WITHIN

A Roadmap to Total Mind, Body,
and Health Transformation

by Kathy Lynn Judson

NAVIGATING THE RACE WITHIN

A Roadmap to Rotal Mind, Body, and Health Transformation

Printed and Electronic Versions
Paperback ISBN: 978-1-956353-49-5
eBook: 978-1-956353-50-1
(Kathy Lynn Judson/Motivation Champs)

The book was printed
in the United States of America.

Special discount may apply on bulk quantities.
Please contact Motivation Champs Publishing to order.
www.motivationchamps.com

DEDICATION

I wanted to reach out to let you know that I have decided to dedicate my book to some very special people in my life. Firstly, I want to dedicate it to my beloved grandfather, who not only shared a birthday with me but also provided unwavering support throughout my journey. Additionally, I would like to dedicate it to three incredible individuals who inspire me daily. Your presence in my life has been invaluable, and I am grateful for your constant encouragement and belief in me.

Thank you all for being the best.

Warm regards,
Kathy

INTRODUCTION

Wow!! I couldn't be happier for you. You have accepted this book and have decided to begin the inside journey of navigating your race within. It is a privilege to accompany you on this exciting adventure. I am interested in hearing about the challenges you faced on your way from being mired in inertia, to pausing, to start anew toward a better future. I want you to have faith in me because I've triumphed through a lot of challenges to get where I am now. Each of you must find your own way through your own unique fate. Mark Twain once observed, "Keep your distance from critics of your objectives. That's what people with weak brainpower are good at, but being among truly exceptional thinkers will inspire you to reach your full potential. I pray that this book encourages you to think big and pushes you to achieve more than you ever thought possible. This book is packed with strategies for regaining control of your life. We'll check out your frame of mind to make sure it's healthy. What you say and what happens to you has tremendous power. Let's make sure that if you approach things with the right frame of mind, nothing can stop you. To reach your lofty goals and become the best version of yourself, you must fuel your body, mind, and spirit. With your selected team by your side, you will be able to do the seemingly impossible. You'll acquire the knowledge necessary to properly fuel your body on a daily basis and, more importantly, before major life events. You'll get an infusion of contagious optimism that will let you explore beneficial new territory in your thinking. Hearing that YOU have found your life's true calling and that your efforts are having an immediate and positive impact on others and preparing you to leave a legacy of which you can be proud will be thrilling. The paths to success and failure look quite similar: However, it is only through taking risks that our circumstances can improve. So, let's get together, face the challenges head-on, and turn them into the foundation for your greatest destiny. I can't contain my enthusiasm for you all. How wonderful that you were picked by You!

TABLE OF CONTENTS

CHAPTER ONE

PREPARATION

It continues to rain heavily; will it ever stop? What about the tent city's resident bikers? Did the floods force them to leave? Oh, and I have some self-doubts. How awfully self-centered! My hotel room is on the second floor, so it's pleasant and warm. There's a storm outside, and I have to ride my mountain bike for 50 miles. Afraid of what the future holds. Exactly why am I putting myself through this? Is it for the sake of glory, or my ego, or am I insane? Sorry, but I must go to bed; I just can't think straight.

After the final wet stage, the day before, all of these things ran through my head while I tried to sleep and recover. Six-inch-deep floods were rushing down the trail, and we had to ride our bikes across them. The most efficient strategy was to keep riding the water for as far as possible. Don't get mired down in the muck; instead, stick to the rivers. After a stormy night at the very tip of the continent, what does today hold? We had a huge wilderness ahead of us, but I'm confident I'm ready for it after all my athletic successes. Ideally, yes. There are still some jitters before each performance, even after all these years.

I got bored of watching golf and tennis a long time ago, in another world. I was twelve years old and had finally had it with my pudgy frame. Thankfully, I developed muscle after reaching adolescence because I am a mesomorph. My new, muscular body was a drastic change from the scrawny kid I used to be. Aspiring to make it big in tennis like Chris Evert. I read somewhere that she needed to be able to run a mile in under six minutes. Despite my certainty that I was doomed to fail, I set out to prove myself wrong. At 12, I decided to stop being so sluggish and start running, and now I'm convinced I can compete in the Olympics. I kept breaking the rules, as women of my era were not permitted to run long distances. In my very rural location, the 800-yard run was the longest event when I was a junior in high school. Now that I'm in my early 60s, I'm thinking about trying to finish a 450-mile mountain bike race in a week. Wow!

What possessed me to break new ground for women in sports? Because men at the time—including my own father—were so quick to say we can't do something. I went out there to prove to them that we could do it if we gave it a shot, so I did. Maybe it was because my dad was stuck in the past and didn't think women could be athletes, or maybe he just didn't think I could. So, I've spent my entire life demonstrating my capability along with so many other pioneering female athletes. Just give US a chance! The state had mandated a mile run for girls by the time I entered high school. I participated in the event and even advanced to the state finals. Being novice coaches unfamiliar with proper race nutrition, they dropped me off at a restaurant to eat a salad. I was a freshman in high school, and this was kind of traumatic. After that poor meal and horrible nutrition, I ended up near the end of the pack. That experience started a quest to learn proper nutrition for racing. The journey to education on how to properly eat before, during and after an event became a priority.

The tragedy of being pushed off the track by an opponent who could not beat me meant that I did not qualify for the states in the mile during my senior year. She pushed me so hard off the track that I fell. What a shock! I picked myself up and placed fourth, but only the top three advanced to the state competition. I was so discouraged that my valedictory address at my high school graduation was on the topic of perseverance. I got many compliments on how I based my presentation around the "Footprints in the Sand" poem. The theme of my life since my loss has been trying to inspire those around me. As long as I can inspire people, I can consider all my lessons in life a real success. Despite this competitor's selfish and immature action by shoving me off the track, I used that action to inspire me to become a top collegiate distance runner. With a couple of great coaches at Colorado State University, I qualified for the National Championships in Cross Country. I couldn't believe it and couldn't wait to get here. My idol, Mary Decker Slaney, was in the same lineup as me, and I couldn't help but be intimidated. From watching her as a 14-year-old Olympian to running with her in person, I was in awe! From that race, I learned that a steady pace, rather than a fast one, is usually the deciding factor in the finish. I just kept pushing and was happy to come in around the middle of the group. WOW!! It was incredible to go from running in the country, where people asked me how I ran so many miles, to racing against dozens of Olympians. I was grateful and kept working hard.

Near the end of my tenure as a collegiate runner, I decided to attempt the Ironman triathlon. I had a dream about it after seeing it on TV. I decided to do the 2.4-mile swim, 112-mile bicycle ride, and full marathon in Kona, Hawaii because if a woman could accidentally cross the finish line and become a hero, then so could I. The woman whose accidental crossing of the finish line inspired me to take up Ironman competition eventually became my teammate in the professional ranks. Here I am, a teammate of the lady who altered the course of my life, just as I once competed against Mary Decker

Slaney and Joan Benoit in college. I referred to fellow triathletes as "tri heads" since we all seemed to have a skewed perception of reality. We were continually tired, yet had another workout to do. As professional triathletes, we dedicated nearly all of our time to both work and training. Most days of the week, I ran between five and ten miles, and I biked between thirty and one hundred miles. Then, four or five times each week, I swam. The training was a lot, indeed!

I got married after playing at the professional level for four years and having an experience of a lifetime. There was a need to adjust the daily training time from five to eight hours. So, I took up bicycle racing. Fortunately, my husband shared my enthusiasm. We went on rides, to races, and on rides with folks who would go on to form the Collegiate Cycling League, all while representing the University of Colorado. What a fantastic time! It was exciting to win two national titles when I was a student at CU. The team's trip to the National Championships was made possible by the women's strong squad. We remain close friends to this day. Since I was committed to my marriage, I also competed in semi-professional races on a national and international level. Many of the other women I knew who pursued professional cycling ended up divorcing their husbands as a result of all the time away and, frankly, their own selfishness. I chose to stay one step below that level and it was still so challenging and rewarding.

My bike took me on a tour of the world. Trying on all the many bicycles available makes me feel like a kid in a candy store. One of the best things about cycling is how many different routes one can take. Every kind of riding brings me closer to nature and gives me a natural high. That high beats out anything I can get from the pharmaceuticals I sell any day. Feelings of strength and wonder are evoked. This level of excitement could lead you to sign up for the most watched mountain bike race in the world, which also happens to be the toughest. Unbelievable! I've gone from being a timid little kid who finished an 800-yard run around a dirt track to a mature athlete who completed the world's longest and most difficult mountain bike race.

What dreams can you accomplish? The choice is up to you! What is your why for working on you?

GOALS + DAILY ACTION = ACHIEVING YOUR DREAMS

Goals are fantastic to have, no matter how big or small. Like getting through the muddiest and rainiest day ever on a bike; I accomplished it. Behind that day were all the smaller goals of riding according to my coach's plan and making healthy lifestyle choices every day.

The human brain is wired to favor routine and an easy way over novelty, even if that routine is unhealthy. Why would anyone eat stale popcorn at a movie? Because at a movie, you eat popcorn, and if it is stale, you still eat it. Crazy! Change your brain and reach your goals and the new destiny that you dream of.

Three tips to trick your brain into novelty and not the old familiar way are:

1. Turn your goal into a habit by engaging the endocannabinoids in your brain to make your goal a habit through consistently using the effects of the endocannabinoids. Yeah, they are like the medical stuff but so much stronger and better, as they work well and precisely.

2. Change your environment. Environmental cues are essential to habit formation, and the brain connects an environment with a specific situation. So, even though the

environment and habit might be totally toxic, your brain goes to the familiar. Change it up! Taking a vacation is the easiest way to change an environment.

3. Use dopamine to your advantage. The feel-good transmitter can be manipulated to allow you to change your behavior and accomplish your goals. If the negative dopamine hits from drugs, illicit sex, porn, or alcohol can give you a buzz and make you feel good, let's use those hits when we accomplish small goals and keep them coming to change a lifestyle to one with healthy horizons long term.

Your Reasons

What's the point of getting up at 4:30–5:00 a.m.?

To get my workout in before work?
Is it because you want to be a healthier, happier you?

Why push yourself to the point of pain? Why, why, why?

Is it for vanity?

To be the most effective, the motivation must come from within you. You are worth it and worthy of the best version of you there is.

Do you push yourself because exercise helps one lose and control weight?

By being more active all day long, the consistency all adds up. You will look better every day.

Is it to stay young as the fear of aging creeps up?

Regular exercise can add years to your life and years off your face.

Is it to be out in nature?

Just breathe in the good and let the stuff go. Exhale out the junk and inhale the great!

Is your doctor ordering it?

Exercise increases the good fats or cholesterol and lowers triglycerides, which are the bad fats in your blood stream, thus helping combat heart disease. Consistent exercise also helps manage health. Won't it be nice to hear the doctor say you have done a great job?

Are you desiring to reach a goal?

Name it, claim it, and see it by putting in the work!

Exercise will give you a boost.

The good brain chemicals—endorphins—produce a rocky mountain high.

Is longevity a primary focus?

Taking care of your body provides better health now and in the future.

Do we strive for an improved immune system?

What is that? Well, that is the way we avoid getting sick.

All the above motivate me every day and have done so for half a century. Yes, that is a long time. You may not be there yet, but let's go to navigating a new healthier you - physically, mentally, and spiritually.

Health and Vitality Declarations

Here is a list of health and vitality declarations to say every day:

- My health is very important to me.
- I have the power to change my story.
- I use my failures as steppingstones.
- I am in awe of what my body is capable of.
- I choose what I become.
- My body is strong.
- I love when my heart works hard.
- I can do anything.
- I feel healthier every day.
- I am strong.
- My strength is greater than any struggle.
- I enjoy perfect health.
- I am stronger than any excuse.
- I inspire others.
- I can, and I will.
- I am grateful that I have the chance to improve.
- I enjoy working out.
- I am amazing.
- I am worth the time, pain, and exertion it takes to have a fit body.
- My body is getting lean, light, fit, and tight.
- I don't stop working out when I am tired but when I am done.

- I believe I can do anything.
- I love being physically fit.
- My body is amazing.
- I am overflowing with happiness.
- I am living stress-free and only in control of me.
- I am well, strong, and thriving.
- I love myself fully.
- I trust my body.
- I am a magnet for health.
- My body is the most precious gift.
- Each day is a gift of life.
- I live each day fully.
- I am brilliant and beautiful.
- I am generous.
- I am attractive.
- I am confident.
- I am open to new ideas.
- I am soaring high.
- I am wealthy.
- I am living where I want to live.
- I am love.
- I have abundance.
- I am filled with honor.
- I am honest and truthful.
- I am prosperous.

- I am courageous.
- I am intelligent and wise.
- I am motivated.
- I am excited about the future.
- I see bright new horizons ahead.
- I am wealthy and successful.
- I am very fortunate.
- I am brilliant and charming.
- I am charismatic and magnificent.
- I am athletic, and I am a highflyer.
- I am intelligent, and I am persistent.
- I am strong and lively.
- I am powerful and magnetic.

Preparation, you'll see in my life it has helped me accomplish things I never dreamed were possible. Preparing for Cape Epic began years ago by the daily routine of proper diet, exercise, and rest. It was a goal for a long time and the daily baby steps to do the race are actions you can do every day also. When I wanted to become a cyclist, I learned about the sport and sought out guidance like this book to propel me to the next stages. Soon after that, I was competing with the best in the world at the time. You can do this in your desired goal wherever you are in life. Just be sure, to prepare your mind, body, and spirit. By taking tips from this chapter and book, you will be on your way to a new healthier horizon. Can you see the new horizon in the distance of your mind? Bring it in and let's work next on focusing on mind, thoughts, and words on the new horizon in our lives.

CHAPTER TWO

The Mindset

Without a dream, you are not living—you are just existing. How does that feel, to exist without a dream? Nothing happens until you start dreaming, and after accomplishing one, you start again to the next one. Everything that has been done and created started with a dream. Dreams, big or small, impact us all.

You were created to dream and dream big! Without a dream, you get stuck. After the great accomplishments one has, it is time to set a new dream. Dreams are built into every cell of your body, and dreams make you a human. Birds can't dream; dogs can't dream; whales can't dream, but a toddler can dream.

What is your dream? The purpose of this chapter is to help you find out and start dreaming and being creative again.

Stage races start as a dream. We watch videos on YouTube and become inspired. We ride trails and think of how they might compare to those of the race we want to do. Cape Epic, the first time, was a dream of about three to four years in the making. This mountain bike stage race is the longest and hardest mountain bike stage race in the world. There is an unspoken competition among multiday races to make them hard. Cape Epic prides itself on being very challenging due to the terrain and the weather. I would throw it out about how cool that would be to do. We would say it would be. Then we would do an easier race, still having our dream on the horizon. Finally, two years later, we got an entry; I calculated the time in Africa to register for an open slot. I had to be up and ready to hit the send button at 3 a.m. I had to be so quick, as people around the world wanted to get in. We were all hitting the send button as fast as we could. Within two minutes, all the open slots were taken. Then you wait to see where you ended up. We ended up getting on the waiting list … So, the dream was still alive. Then we had to trust the process, and this was pre-covid. We didn't get into the Covid year, but it was great, as they canceled the race after everyone was there. So, we were in the US, just riding and chilling. And those that went lost their spot and a bunch of money.

Our dream was still alive for the next year that we banked the entry for. Life happened, and distractions got in the way of the dream. At the somewhat last minute, we had to give up this entry. I ended up letting the race have it back to give to someone else to allow them to have a dream come true. It was such a hard race to gain entry into, so we paid forward for our own slot. When I was able to secure our slot, I thought, *I am not waiting until two months before go time to get an invite!* I found you could buy an entry by sponsoring any one of several organizations. It was hard to choose which one mainly because of not knowing who to sponsor or support and what their requirements were. By grace, I picked the Cancer Society of South Africa, and a phenomenal person named Johan responded. We were so blessed to be chosen by Johan. He got us an entry from one of the volunteers. That entry paid for four months of work for the volunteer, and it gave us the opportunity to get into the Cape Epic. We were in!

After four years of trying, we had an entry into the Big Dance!

I wanted to jump for joy! Then we commenced the task of daily putting in the work to prepare for the toughest mountain bike race in the world. We often looked at the course profiles and wondered if we could do it. So, we kept watching videos and training. We did some great rides in the cold. They were perfect prep for the mud stage. Then it was go-time, and we relied on all that we had done.

Declarations and a Confidence Board

Let's focus on declarations and a confidence board to produce the changes you want to make happen in your own life toward becoming healthier, wealthier, and wiser.

Both excellent tools are components to begin transforming your mindset into a powerful, magnetic one! This all takes time, repetition, and a goal of what you want to be.

When the pain of not being where you want to be is great enough, you will jump at the opportunity to change.

Declarations are statements said with confidence and belief. They have helped thousands. Declarations work because they can reprogram your mind into believing what you say. Our minds cannot tell the difference between real and fantasy, like when we are watching a movie.

How can we work toward making declarations more effective and powerful?

- ◆ Write out your negative qualities you and others point out. Look for a common theme, and then you can make a shift.

- ◆ Write a positive declaration on the positive aspect of your self-judgment. Use a thesaurus to find more powerful words to make your statements more robust.

- Speak the declarations out loud for five to 10 minutes three or four times a day or write them out several times a day in a journal with belief and feelings.

- Have someone else repeat the declarations to you or record your own voice to listen and believe what you hear.

Declarations can be a tremendous tool to help you change your mood or state of mind and manifest the changes you want to see.

CREATING A CONFIDENCE BOARD

The second focal point in this chapter will be creating a confidence board. They are so important to take the time to do, as this will make your dreams real. "Creating a confidence board is probably one of the most valuable visualization tools available to you," says Jack Canfield.

Creating a confidence board allows you to focus on positive thoughts and bring them to life in the real world.

Let's get started!

Your confidence board is your powerful tool to visualize your dreams and life's desires.

Our attitudes and beliefs create a magnet to attract events, circumstances, and opportunities for us to live out those attitudes and beliefs.

Creating a confidence board is a tool to turn your greatest dreams into reality. A confidence board helps you narrow down your desires through the power of choice. This tool helps you invest the time and energy into visualizing your future and consistently reminds you of your life goals.

A confidence board is so powerful because it forces you to make choices and find clarity. You must figure out your own desires and focus on those that are important to you. The limited space forces you and empowers you to focus on what you genuinely want. This is a simple yet meaningful tool. By selecting the right pictures, you are focusing on the details of how to represent your desire. By focusing on the choices, you send your mind extremely specific and personalized messages.

The power of visualization is so underestimated. When we see something, it works on our mind and brain to make it a reality. Our brain tries to make us successful with every action we take. Our brains train our bodies to act. When we imagine ourselves preparing for an activity, our brains run through the event and send signals to the rest of our body to complete the action. If done properly, visualization is ALMOST as powerful as performing the action. When you visualize yourself doing something you really want to accomplish and can play it as a movie, your brain trains your body for that reality.

Consistency is important. We learn by repetition after the age of seven. Every time we repeat an action, we become stronger with that action. I use visualization often in bicycle racing. The clearer the picture I can get, the better the race goes. By creating a confidence board and placing it in a place you can see every day, you create the opportunity for consistent visualization to retrain your mind, body, and spirit to manifest your desires.

The initial creation of the board takes time and energy, but after that, consistency and visualization happen every time you look at it.

Let us start making that board and creatively have some FUN!

Step 1: Figure out and plan YOUR board. Take some time to thoughtfully consider the message you want your personalized board to say and how you want it to look. The following questions will help organize the plan:

- Which of your true wishes and desires do you want to reflect on your confidence board? Think about your values, career goals, family life, love life, health, wellness, how you spend your free time, and what you want to learn and grow into. Answer these questions first and then begin selecting your images.

- Do you want one board or multiple boards for different areas of your life? When making this decision, realize that you will need to place this board in a visible area, specifically one that you can see every day.

- What type of images will you use (printed or actual photographs)? What will be the source (e.g., newspapers, magazines, images/quotes from the Internet, your Pinterest board, photographs, book pages, brochures/pamphlets/flyers)? Choose your images wisely, as these are a major component of your confidence board. Will your confidence board be tidy or messy?

- Do you want your board to feature several declarations?

- Do you want to add decorative elements or embellishments so your board will fit in with your decor?

Step 2: Buy your supplies and gather your confidence board images.

Step 3: Set up your space, as this is a very personal experience. It's time to get in touch with your true self, identify your true desires, and focus your energy on attracting them into your life. This is something you are doing for yourself. From a quiet and uninterrupted space, create your board, making it all about you and what you want for your life. Make sure you have a few hours all by yourself to really focus on this special gift to yourself.

Work in an inviting work environment with proper lighting, music, and smells to use all the senses that you have so your entire being gets involved in the energizing process. Turn on the music. Play your special music that really lights up your soul. If you get distracted by the lyrics, then find some nice instrumental music to play. Pray or meditate before you begin. Take some time to sit quietly and check in with how you are feeling. Let go of all your worries about the day. These moments are all that matters right now. Be present in the now to have your brain record more to create a more lasting memory.

Step 4: Finally, *it is time to create your confidence board.* Let your creative power shine. It is entirely up to you how it turns out. It is YOUR board. What matters is the images mirror YOUR desires. When you look at the board's images, you should feel a strong connection to those desires. Take time to cut your images out. Sit with your images for a moment before you attach them to your board. Hold them in your hand and gaze upon them. Feel the desire running through your body. Notice what emotions arise when you think of that image and the desires that it conjures. See yourself getting what you want and feel the happiness radiating from it. How you feel right now is what you want to feel every time you look at your confidence board.

Once you have created your confidence board, place it in an area where you see it at least daily. The refrigerator door is a great space. Additionally, sit with it at least once a week for at least 10 minutes to visualize what you want. Revisit the feelings of happiness and gratitude for eventually having those desires in your life.

Your confidence board is a wonderful reminder of what you truly want in life. It is a powerful motivator to get you to act on achieving your goals. Treat your confidence board as if it is very sacred. It is a special and powerful tool to attract all your desires into your life.

The Power of a Confidence Board

Tony Robbins, a world-renowned peak performance coach, has famously said when talking about the importance of moving toward your goals and dreams that if you aren't growing, you are dying.

By paying attention to your dreams and taking the time to shape them into concrete aspirations, you are taking a step toward moving yourself in the direction of growth and away from the alternative.

Napoleon Hill, the famous author of one of the most popular personal development books of all time, *Think and Grow Rich*, said, "Man, alone, has the power to transform his thoughts into physical reality; man, alone, can dream and make his dreams come true."

He has gone on to say, "Thoughts are things." The importance of paying attention to your desires and treating them seriously cannot be overstated.

A confidence board is a concrete representation of your desires and aspirations for a compelling life. They are fun to create and can serve as an invaluable tool to motivate and inspire you toward concrete daily action in pursuit of your biggest and most important life goals.

With a confidence board in hand, you will be moving toward growth in the most key areas of your life!

Using a Confidence Board to Manifest Your Dreams

With your confidence board created, the next crucial step is to ensure that you are utilizing your creation to its fullest extent. The following tips can help you maximize the impact your vision board will make on your life:

1. Look at your confidence board daily.
   The magic of a confidence board is not just in the process of creating one, but it is in the daily reminders it can provide you to remember and work toward your dreams.

2. Place your confidence board where you will see it daily. Ideally, first thing in the morning and in the evening before bedtime.

3. Notice as you make progress toward your dreams. Progress toward your dreams will happen if you give it time, put in your full effort, and pay attention to signals in your life that demonstrate that you are moving in a positive direction.
   A powerful technique is to keep a confidence journal, where you can write down your thoughts and make a note of any signs that you are moving toward your dreams.

Celebrate success!

When you notice progress toward your vision, make sure to celebrate it! Perhaps you have a goal to increase your income by 20% and have noticed that you were able to score a nice promotion at work that puts you part of the way toward your goals. Leo Babauta, the author of the top personal development site Zenhabits.net, has written about the importance of celebrating success in motivating you toward a goal. **"Every little step along the way is a success—celebrate the fact that you even started!"** Celebrate every achievement. The more you celebrate your successes, both big and small, the more progress you will notice in pursuit of your vision, and the more motivated you will feel to continue your journey.

Once all the goals have been achieved on that vision board, it's time to make a new one that keeps you focused on extending your life large.

A confidence board will catapult your dreams into reality.

To realize a dream, you need to have a clear vision. By creating a confidence board, you are clarifying your vision. The vision board builds your confidence, as you see the end product on display and can stay focused on your goals. Your brain needs an intention to have faith in yourself as well as act toward making abstract ideas and dreams come to life. A vision board is a great tool to increase your dreams and expectations. Declarations added to a vision board help recreate a mindset. The power of words is phenomenal. Words are energy and speaking what you start the process of preparing your mind for the realization of your dream. Words and mindset also start the processes of bringing forces together to bring your dreams to pass. For example, today on my ride, I was slogging it along and wanted to go faster. I said it sure would be nice to have someone to ride with to go faster. Low and behold, a younger woman was there beside me and we had a lovely little ride encouraging each other onward. The power of a vision, words, and a proper mindset is phenomenal.

You are never too old to set a new goal or to dream a new dream. For broken dreams, the cure is to dream again and deeper. "This is where dreams—dreams, do you understand—come to life, come real"

(C. S. Lewis, author of *Chronicles of Narnia*).

CHAPTER THREE

The Power of Words
Learn to Love Yourself

———————

There is always more to you than meets the eye. Even when things are extremely challenging, it can help to keep telling oneself encouraging statements. The challenge may be physical, mental, or emotional. The intellect needs to be coaxed into harmony with the body and the emotions.

Early in the day, it poured, but eventually the rain stopped. The atmosphere was peaceful and hopeful. With any luck, the rain will stop. Over my left shoulder, a rainbow appeared. After 12 hours of nonstop rain, I was hoping it would finally stop. We were at the furthest end of the continent, so how could it have lasted so long? The first rays of sunshine encouraged us as we began to climb the first hill. At this time, the trail was muddy but still rideable. Not quite as slow as riding a river, but still not fast. The sky suddenly began to pour down rain. Storm after storm of the kind I'd never dare ride through. It was a windy day. People in front of me kept falling off their bikes because they were unable to ride. A very long day has just begun. Not much food remained by the time we reached the first water stop. I decided to use a trash bag as an umbrella and blanket.

When and how should a trash bag be worn? How big of a bag would you recommend? A trash bag of 55 gallons will do as a makeshift raincoat. I can't figure out how to get my arms and helmet through. A trash bag is completely impenetrable. The volunteer, a fantastic South African man with enormous energy, understood my mission, and he graciously assisted me. A proper raincoat was created by us. To have made a nice raincoat that does its job as intended is to have made a proper raincoat. Knowing it would be another long day in the saddle, I was back on the path again as quickly and as hard as I could go.

The rainbow has disappeared. Nothing except clouds and water for what seems like forever. The slick muck that blocked your bike's gears was cruel, measuring in at inches deep. Bikes were breaking down and people were losing them. I just kept going and pedaled carefully so as not to damage the chain. It was during one of these times that I wished for my partner's strength. Due to a medical emergency (extreme dehydration), he had to drop out of the competition. I needed his reassurance and encouragement so badly. When one of us was struggling, the other would step in to help, and vice versa. He was now a spectator. I could sense his power, but he wasn't the one slogging in the muck with me. Despite the chill, I was relieved to know he was inside where it was secure and warm. I'd keep going and rely on the routines I've developed through many years of surviving in hazardous environments. Once, while competing in a race, I rode through a snowfall that dumped five inches of snow on us. It had been decades since I'd faced such adversity, but I knew I could draw strength from the memory and fortitude I'd accumulated then as though it were yesterday. We were on the go for a total of eight hours. Seeing people who had given up ahead of me gave me the push I needed to keep going. If you stopped, you'd be stuck there for hours, shivering. Just get to the next aid station, and the one after that, and so on. If you want to avoid falling behind in energy, eat as much as you can stomach. Being so chilly prevented me from eating. I only succeeded in eating the gels.

After seven hours of drudgery, we spotted the final rise in the distance. It was gruesome! It was a very long, very steep climb. I was hoping there might be a route we could use to get to the end. But no! The organizers truly made this an amazing experience by making us wade through a muck for six miles. So off we went, either riding or sliding. The time limit was rapidly approaching, so we had to exert maximum effort. The final three kilometers were in a slick bog through which no vehicle could pass. I realized then that I was doomed to fail. I decided to just let the Cape Epic lion tame me. All I wanted was a hug and to see my partner's beautiful smile. At long last, I arrived. My race plate was cut off, and I was over. I was defeated, but I knew that on that one terrible, unpleasant day, I had given it everything I had.

After a relaxing hour in the hot shower, I enjoyed a delicious meal with my great and powerful companion. A miracle occurred while we were eating! The time limit for finishing the event has been changed. After a little setback, I was once again in the running. The hyenas, the riders who stayed behind to ensure the last riders crossed the finish line, complained to the race directors that the day's conditions were the worst they had experienced in seven years. With each new round of rain, the track became increasingly treacherous. On the fifty-mile circuit, we rode and slogged through torrential downpours, mud up to our knees, and washed-out roads. Everyone who made it through that section deserves a medal of some sort. The ups and downs of feeling were extreme. It was incredible to go from complete hopelessness to mustering the will to fight for even one more day. I still had one more day to complete the toughest race I'd run in 30 years.

That was a long time ago, before I became a mother, before I started my work, before my life took on its current form. That night, I saw a rainbow over the water with my great companion. It was lovely and comfortable. Thank goodness for that beautiful rainbow over the South Atlantic. Both the morning and evening rainbows foretold fresh starts the next day.

LIFE DOES NOT JUST HAPPEN TO YOU. THAT IS WHY I ENJOY THE FOLLOWING QUOTES AS THEY INSPIRE ME TO KEEP WORKING WELL AT MY OWN LIFE AND TO REALIZE I OVERSEE MY OWN DESTINY.

Life does not happen to you! It happens for you!

"Talk to yourself like someone who you love." —Brene Brown

"If you are always trying to be normal, you will never know how amazing you can be." —Dr. Maya Angelou

"We have the need to be accepted and to be loved by others, but we cannot accept and love ourselves. The more self-love we have, the less we will experience self-abuse. Self-abuse comes from self-rejection, and self-rejection comes from having an image of what it means to be perfect and never measuring up to that ideal." —Don Miguel Ruiz

Self-harming behaviors, getting involved with people who treat us poorly, pushing away people who treat us well, and ingesting harmful substances are some of the obvious forms of self-rejection.

"Love yourself so much that when someone treats you wrong, you recognize it." —Rena Rosa

(Avoid the self-rejection of staying with those who treat us poorly while pushing away those who treat us well.)

We want to begin the journey from surviving to thriving—we want to overcome self-rejection that we have carried too long, love ourselves, and change our perspective to be the best that we can become. We must nourish each aspect of our lives. The ways that we limit, reject, and sell ourselves short are endless, and the result is that we feel less than whole and less than fulfilled.

When you are stuck in a rut, it is easy to blame an event, someone else, or yourself. Does that change anything? No! Your real choices are to change your life, change your own tapestry to match where you are now, or retool your life to match the dreams and visions of the future. Changing our perspective is such an incredible journey. It helps us find our purpose and what we were created to become.

What got you to the point where you recognized the need for change as commonly caused by feeling stuck or a sense of emptiness? We were at the top, never quite satisfied, and sold our souls out to move ahead, pleasing everyone but ourselves and living in the future and not now. This brings us to the awareness of a rudder adjustment. To live life with a new sense of purpose, we need to set our priorities. Put first things first and do not get drifting downwind.

Living by your beliefs and values will enable you to make decisions based on those. One of your goals should be to always live by your beliefs and values to have the most integrity in yourself and earn the trust and respect of others. Making sure we are daily living by our values assures that we will have a clear conscience and spend more time listening to our inner voice and not being influenced by others.

Won't it be amazing to wake up every day and anticipate what the day holds? When we are living with purpose, we put our whole heart into everything we do. Living a life following our passion also helps us feel that we are making a difference in our own little world. Act and dream as if you will live forever but live as if you will die right now.

Live with a feeling of contentment and inner peace. The grass is greener under your own two feet as you make the lush pasture.

When we find our purpose, we make a meaningful difference in others' lives. As an old proverb says, "A candle loses nothing by lighting another candle."

Living in the moment allows us to cherish the moments and live a life without regrets. Dr. Seuss said it best: "Do not cry because it's over. Smile because it happened."

Success in life begins with purpose. When you achieve clarity, you will have a new perspective. You will feel good about who you are, what you stand for, and where you are going. You will have an inner peace that will replace your need to seek approval from others. Others will notice the new you: someone who is happy, motivated, and self-assured. You will be a new, powerful, magnetic you. The purpose of our life is to live a life of purpose. The time to start is now. It is never too late.

When you find yourself lost or depressed, then your life doesn't match your own unique tapestry. Drugs or alcohol won't get you to your dreams, and they only are ways to reject you—the beautiful person you are. They only numb you from seeing what you can change. So, the first thing to do is recognize that you're stuck in a rut, then dig deeper until you realize your deepest needs. Once those deepest needs are in focus, you can create a new mosaic that blends perfectly on the way to a revitalized life.

You Need a Purpose!

To start to change who you are, these five areas need attention:

- Take control of your mind or focus. FEED your mind instead of feeding on the weeds all around you. Daily stand guard at the door of your mind, and just like your body, feed it daily at a minimum of an hour per day. We are what we read, listen to, and watch. Say your affirmations daily with emotions.

- Feed and strengthen your body. PUSH yourself. Don't settle. GET PHYSICAL. Get an hour of power going.

- Get a ROLE MODEL to give you inspiration to a pathway to get you to where you want to be. Have a coach like me or have a mentor.

- MAKE A PLAN and start massive action. Just get moving! Try something else.

- FEED and strengthen your spirit.

- Be grateful for what you have and start giving to those less fortunate than you are. You can have an influence on others' lives.

Here are additional thoughts and ideas on how to change YOUR beautiful tapestry of life.

Our stories are stored in the neurons in our brains, and to address those, we each must look at the thoughts and emotions behind them as we did in the last module. The key is to recognize that your stories are keeping you from the beautiful mosaic of a life you want and preventing you from leaving a legacy.

Do our stories and ruts keep us locked into failure, or is it more like "Hey, I am comfortable as is"? A personal example follows. I held on to an 'I am not good enough' mindset. It was a shield, a buffer to prevent failure in life, athletics, and relationships. I grew up with it as it was shown to me by my childhood role models. Did it serve me later in life? No! So, what is not serving me had to be released. Working diligently on the above five core ideas to change and hugging my inner little girl, I am continuing the awesome journey to a powerful and magnetic *me*! Recognizing that I could be so much more valuable to myself, the people in my life, and the world at large has been a huge blessing. Like tiles in a larger mosaic, those old pieces are part of the fabric, but now they are overshadowed by many more beautiful and colorful tiles. The old is no longer seen, as the new vibrant tiles are shining too brightly.

I have become confident and have inner peace. Thanks to great friends, mentors, and learning tools to live a more powerful and positive life, I ride the wave of life again.

It is your turn now! Let's work together to tap into your creative power to create the life you want to live. We need to get the momentum started with the following steps. Ready, set, GO!

1. What do you love to do that goes easy and flows from within? Write it down. Somewhere along your journey, you lose sight of how amazing your life can be because of the burdens of responsibilities and the mundane of life. Forget that old way and reconnect with what brings you joy and what you love. For me, that is cycling, windsurfing, yoga, and skiing. I started riding my bike more, have been windsurfing until my arms couldn't lift a sail, and just kept hitting it. Please do not ever stop doing the things that make you feel happy and alive.

    Age is only important if you are wine and cheese. I haven't let a few years slow me down. Life is short. Live it to the fullest. Throw away every stinking excuse you are telling yourself right now: no money, no time, no resources, etc. GO FIND A WAY! Commit YOURSELF to doing what you love to do and watch the story of your life BLOSSOM.

2. Become an ADVENTURER. Explore the world to tap into your flow and get in touch with who YOU ARE. You will have time to focus on yourself and gain a new perspective. By going on adventures, you will gain clarity on who you are, where you are going, and what you want to accomplish, and you will leave a legacy at the same time.

3. After your grand adventure, you can reconnect with YOUR dreams and GO for it. Dream big! What did you want to do in life before the mundane took over? Start writing in your journal and connect with the dreams you had once upon a time in a galaxy far, far away. Make new DREAMS. If you lived in a perfect world, what would you do, love to be, or have?

4. Finding your new dreams and motivation will allow you to grow and stretch. Jump out of that lobster pot and expand your comfort zone regularly. Try new things and meet new people. Growth doesn't happen if you sit and wait for it to happen. Do something slightly dangerous yet invigorating. Get into the zone where you are stretching just enough to continue to grow and evolve.

5. Get quiet, relax, and listen. When you are quiet and listening, pay attention to the signs on the roads, radio songs, and the people you meet. All of these are your messengers with divine guidance to give you a nice gentle kick in the backside to move you forward along your path.

6. You are powerful and magnetic, and YOU can create the life you desire. You have the power to be, have, and do anything you desire. Make it happen. Start studying the law of attraction and put it into practice for 21 days. Journal your life as you move forward. When we are stuck and lost, we forget that we choose what we think and how we feel.

By using daily declarations, meditation, positive movements, and journaling as examples, it's important to be grateful for the joy and beauty around you. With gratitude, you are open to receiving more love, grace, and beauty in new and amazing ways.

7. Ask for help! Ask for help from a life coach, mentor, friend, counselor, or God Himself. Having a chat with someone may just give you the necessary ideas for YOUR greatness.

I want to leave you with 10 lessons that will make you a better person:

- Ignoring your gut instinct can get you into trouble.
- If you can't be kind, be kind.
- When you lie, the truth will eventually come to the surface.
- Worrying is a waste of time. It steals your peace, and most of the time, it doesn't happen.
- Don't raise your voice. Improve your argument.
- Don't rush. Trust the timing of your life.
- Be strong enough to let go of the things that make you unhappy.
- Worrying about what people think is like putting your soul in prison.

- A negative mind will never give you a positive life.
- Talk about your blessings more than your problems.

Now here's some great mindset-changing work for you to do: This looks daunting in a way, but YOU are worth the time you invest in yourself.

- Write out your story and your dreams to gain clarity and self-knowledge. This makes us aware of deeply buried pieces of ourselves that affect our decisions, engagement with life, choice of work, and every relationship we have. When our pieces are brought from darkness to light, we can see change. This may be a slow and painful process, yet it is necessary. When we have a greater awareness of ourselves, we gain a greater acceptance of ourselves and others. We all have a story to share that may just help others see their worth and value. LET'S DO IT!

- Create five new stories or envision ones you knew before. Do this in a new way. Write them down to bring inspiration. Make them as detailed as possible and feel the emotions involved. Then play them in your mind daily until they happen.

- Do your daily affirmations and update them as needed.

- Fill out your DAILY PERSONAL ORGANIZER.

- Get some other support besides this course and make connections that will last as the changes heal you.

- Find others who will support you, keeping you on track and self-disciplined. This course can do some of that, yet it is good to develop other support systems as well.

- Take accountability. We will walk together to keep you

accountable and can be that partner to hold you true to your own commitments, allowing you to make the changes you want to make.

- Forgive. Accepting others as they are and forgiving others helps us accept and forgive ourselves. We learn from our mistakes. Who can you forgive? Who can you accept as they are in your life?

- As mentioned earlier, who is your mentor going to be? Who will model new things for you and show you how to do them?

- Journal your successes every day!

- You will have fellow traveling companions on the journey to a new, powerful, and magnetic YOU! In the FB group, you can partner with others to support, influence, and learn from one another. There is such power in groups like this when the intention is to assist one another in the positive change to a new, wonderful, and powerful you!

When we are stuck, growth and transformation are arrested. When you do the same old patterns repeatedly, you remain stuck. Do you want to continue going around the same problem over and over or move up to a higher destiny?

EACH DAY, OUR GOAL IS TO BE NEW AND IMPROVED!

Self-image Declarations:

- I am now confident and assertive.
- I am growing more and more attractive every day.
- I value honesty and truth.
- I am now a powerful and charismatic personality.

- I am confident in the presence of others.
- I am not afraid to be wrong.
- I enjoy honest people.
- I walk and move with assurance, poise, and personal power.
- I am growing more and more attractive every day.
- I am now friendly, outgoing, and confident.
- I move my body with poise and confidence.
- I hold myself and other people in high esteem.
- My confident energy, enthusiasm, and passion are increasing massively every day.
- I am now bold and courageous. I now seize my opportunities immediately.
- I have the ability to change anything in my life that I choose to change. I take complete responsibility for my life.
- I can now create a state of total certainty and confidence at a moment's notice anytime I need it.
- What I imagine I can do, I can do.
- I am now fearless, courageous, and bold.
- I receive wisdom and knowledge from my subconscious mind every moment of my life.
- I am getting stronger every day.
- My confident energy, enthusiasm, and passion are increasing massively every day.
- I now see myself as the person I want to be: confident, self-assured, healthy, and prosperous.
- I now apply my faith with consistent acts of courage.

- I am now positively adventurous and outgoing.

- I now put myself into new, positive, and challenging situations daily.

- My thoughts, presence, charm, and charisma now inspire others to gain greater self-confidence and personal power.

- When I speak, the tone of my voice communicates strength, courage, and confidence.

- I am now confident, assertive, and decisive in every situation.

- I dare to be different.

- I am now an outstanding leader who leads with confidence.

- Other people find me a fascinating and interesting person.

- I consciously choose the emotional state I am always in.

- I am now raising my standards in all the major areas of my life and always holding myself to those standards.

- I act as if I already have all the confidence I need and desire.

- I choose what I become.

- I am brave enough to climb any mountain.

- No one can make me feel inferior.

Character Declarations

- Having integrity is having strong moral principles and core values. You follow your principles, whether people are watching or not.

- Being honest is living the truth. It is being authentic and trustworthy in all your interactions, relationships, and thoughts. It requires self-honesty.

- Being loyal is being faithful and devoted to your loved ones, your friends, and anyone you have a trusted relationship with.

- I treat each person with courtesy, kindness, dignity, and deference, as each person is unique and wonderful.

- In each area of my life, I meet and exceed my responsibilities.

- I am grateful for my many blessings, and I am content.

- Today, I seek to alleviate the suffering of another.

- I will use my discernment, integrity, and compassion to make fair decisions today.

- Please forgive me. I am sorry. I love you. Thank you!

- Walking in authenticity in every moment allows others to trust me.

- I have the courage to embrace and overcome obstacles set before me.

- I am generous with all I have and expect nothing in return.

- I have the perseverance to reach my goals.

- My self-esteem gives me the grace to act politely to others and myself.

- My positive view of life allows me to be kind to others.

- I act in a certain manner, showing love in words, actions, and expressions to those I deeply care about.

- My world is amazing in every area of my life.

- I do what I say I will do.

- I do the best I can in every endeavor.

- I am using my strong self-discipline to achieve my desired goals.

'I Am' Declarations:

- I am generous.
- I am attractive.
- I am confident.
- I am open to new ideas.
- I am soaring high.
- I am wealthy.
- I am living where I want to live.
- I am love.
- I am abundant.
- I am filled with honor.
- I am honest.
- I am truthful.
- I am prosperous.
- I am courageous.
- I am intelligent.
- I am wise.
- I am motivated.
- I am excited.
- I am rich.
- I am a superstar.
- I am fortunate.

- I am brilliant.
- I am charming.
- I am wonderful.
- I am beautiful.
- I am charismatic.
- I am magnificent.
- I am jubilant.
- I am an overachiever.
- I am a highflyer.
- I am athletic.
- I am happy.
- I am successful.
- I am joyful.
- I am persistent.
- I am strong.
- I am lively.
- I am powerful.

The Gift of Giving

Give out of love, not obligation
Give when it's least expected
Give without strings attached
Give from your heart
Give of yourself
Give to show that you care
Give help without causing helplessness
Give something that takes personal sacrifice
Give to make a difference

Give without keeping score
Give for no reason at all
Give a little if you can't give a lot
Give without attracting attention to yourself
Give without being asked
Give of your experience
Give to those who need it most
(Frank Sonnenberg)

Always keep expecting, as there is power in expectations. Expect the unexpected! Prepare for the unexpected like making a proper raincoat out of a 55-gallon trash bag. Don't develop your expectations based on others' beliefs and opinions, as they might limit all you are capable of. Your expectations drive your beliefs. I expected to finish the Cape Epic race from the time I signed up three years prior to doing it. I just knew I would. So, my past and the expectations of others did not phase me as I stayed in the moment and expected to finish one day at a time. Don't limit your expectations by basing them on past performances. Stay your course right now toward your expectations. Your beliefs become your behaviors, and your behaviors become your habits. If you live your life through awesome habits, your limitless expectations can become a reality. Keep expecting the unexpected and believe that what you declare will come to pass. That is the value of declarations. They build up your expectations and your beliefs so that all things become possible!

CHAPTER FOUR

All the Fruits of Tomorrow are in the Seeds of Today

The topic of food and nutrition is fraught with prejudice. You need it to stay alive and prosper. Excessive amounts of food cause serious problems for the body. Obesity is indirectly related to 80 percent of the healthcare expenditures in the country. Yet, if there isn't enough food a person does not thrive well. Our culture has some rather strange views on a substance that sustains life. Some people eat it to ease their nerves or divert their attention from their emotions. They soothe themselves in eating "comfort foods." As commonly as people turn to drink or narcotics to ease the pain of past trauma, so do people turn to food. Either eating too much or not enough will accomplish the diversion of navigating the race within themselves.

Just recently, I experienced a watershed moment in my own life. Since I was 16 years old, I have battled an eating disorder. It certainly has not been a journey that I wanted to endure, but it has been mine. As Brene Brown says, "You either walk inside your story and own it or you stand outside your story and hustle for your worthiness." I chose and chose to dive deep to my story. That's why it's crucial that we put the past to rest... Looking at old photos from Cape Epic, I realized that my legs and hips are in fantastic shape. Although I have skinny arms, the rest of my body is built like a cyclist's. While my larger hips and powerful legs may make me look like I have tree trunks for legs, they are the source of my strength and power. A word, indeed! A solid base is the source of lasting strength and power. The daily weather attacks on a 60-story structure necessitate an extremely wide and deep base. The same as me in an African stage race. I required that solid groundwork to endure anything the mountains of Colorado or Africa would throw at me. I will never win a contest on being like Twiggy, yet I have won many contests climbing tall mountains. That is my story.

Some opt for surgery to change aspects of themselves they desire to enhance, reduce, or alter. Surgery to narrow my hips is out of the question. I can get my genetic fat reduced, but not my hip structure. As a result of owning my story, I am appreciative of the fantastically powerful body I was given at birth, which enables me to compete successfully and finish some of the world's most grueling races.

It's a bummer that I'm still struggling with anorexia and bulimia after all these years. I've been at a perfectly normal weight for decades. I am 5 feet, 7 inches tall and weigh 120 pounds. I am not fat at all! But I still struggle at times because of the social stigmas associated with women's body images and the lasting mental repercussions of anorexia and bulimia. Now, I know what triggers me, like when ladies who are self-conscious about their body want to show them off. When I start to go there, I must pause and tell myself, "No!" What you do every day is impossible for others to accomplish. I would rather have powerful legs and a strong body instead of being so weak that I can't even pick up my gear required for the sports I participate in. Grace, gratitude, and determination will help me keep my strength, health, and fitness.

That's what I wish for each of you, too. When you go into a room with the confidence of a rock star, that's because you are a rock star.

You have a lot of charm. Please keep it in mind always. You are loved more deeply than you realize. Even if you feel like you must start from scratch every time. You will see the logic behind everything that has transpired one day. Stay true to who you are. Love fiercely always. Keep risking everything, even if your heart keeps breaking, because the world needs you just as you are. The daily uphill climb is well worth it if the reward at the summit is a clear view of a bright future.

REFUSE TO SETTLE.

This chapter was challenging to write because there is so much information on nutrition and exercise out there. One size does not fit all, and there is always something to learn.

I am a proponent of just doing something. I love activities done outdoors (e.g., cycling, skiing, windsurfing, SUP, yoga, hiking). I am unique and am very grateful to live in Colorado, where I can just go. My point is that you must find something YOU want to do and enjoy doing. Get outside, stay inside, or take a walk. JUST MOVE.

This will be the basics about starting a routine after we delve into fueling your body.

There is a myriad of diets out there, but it comes down to basic principles, which I will focus on next. Your body needs to be in the best condition possible so that your mind and body can propel you to the life of your dreams and visions.

The science of it is that your body requires certain chemicals to function—water, minerals, vitamins, and amino acids—which are all obtained from carbohydrates, fats, and protein. Without one of those in the right amount, you will cease to exist. There are thousands of combinations, and some are better than others. In a future course, we will explore more about nutrition. For our purposes now, it is hoped that I give you a jump start on a new way of living. Thus, we start at the very beginning.

Resources about nutrition abound. For elementary principles, the www.HHS.gov website has many outstanding articles. A Google search for basic nutrition principles is another great resource.

How Do You Eat Healthy?

Take your changes in small steps. It is like the mindset work we started earlier and continue to do.

From the 2015–2020 dietary guidelines for Americans, you get to make the choices that help you reach or keep a healthy body weight, get the nutrients you need, and lower your risk of certain diseases. The primary point is to eat a variety of foods and beverages that are nutritious.

You need to eat from all the good groups:

- Vegetables (lots of colors)
- Fruits (especially whole fruits)
- Grains (especially whole grains)
- Fat-free and low-fat dairy, including milk, yogurt, and cheese.
- Protein from seafood and lean meats

Even within each group, switch it up and eat a wide variety.

After learning about the food groups, it is time to learn about what you need to eat calorically to maintain or lose weight. This is dependent upon how active you are, your age, your sex, your height, and your weight. Two easy calculators are www.choosemyplate.gov/ calculator and myfitnesspal.com. Both works well, and my personal preference is www.myfitnesspal.com or www.Lifesum.com. Both are great apps for tracking nutrition and exercise.

To assist you in achieving your goals, you should limit foods and beverages high in saturated fats, added sugars, and sodium. Less than 10 percent of calories should arise from saturated fats, and less than 10 percent of the calories should come from sugars. Also, limit your sodium intake to under two grams.

Stick with it and feel better every day. Use these eight healthy eating goals for additional support:

- Make half of your plate fruits and vegetables. Choose red, orange, and dark-green veggies like tomatoes, sweet potatoes, and broccoli. Add fruit as part of the main or side dishes or as a dessert. The more colorful your plate, the more likely you are to get the vitamins, minerals, and fiber your body needs to be healthy.

- Make half the grains you eat whole grains. Switch to whole-grain foods. Look for whole wheat, brown rice, bulgur, buckwheat, oatmeal, rolled oats, quinoa, and wild rice.

- Switch to fat-free or low-fat milk. Get the same calcium and other essential nutrients as whole milk with fewer calories and less saturated fats.

- Compare sodium content in foods and choose lower-sodium versions: low-sodium, reduced-sodium, or no-salt options.

- Choose a variety of lean proteins (e.g., lean meats, poultry, seafood, dry beans or peas, eggs, nuts, and seeds).

- Drink water instead of sugary drinks.

- Eat some seafood. Shoot eight ounces a week or four ounces twice a week.

- Cut back on solid fats (e.g., cakes, cookies, pizza, hot dogs, bacon, ribs, and ice cream).

Here are some more great tips that you can use as well:

- Mix veggies into your go-to dishes.

- Handy snack: Use cut-up fruit and veggies.

- WATER is a staple of snack time.

- Cookie monster gets to hand out fresh fruit.

- Bake or grill food.

- Drink water and fat-free milk as your go-to drinks.

- Serve fruit as a dessert.

- Don't add salt.

- Use smaller plates.

- Keep portion sizes appropriate for age, gender, and activity level.

- Balance calories: know what you need and track your intake.

- Enjoy your food but eat less.

- Get some massive momentum going; have physical exercise be a part of your everyday routine.

- I am adding a lot of tips, as I want to present many so that you can select as many as you can that resonate with you:

- Cook a big batch of grain or beans once a week as a basis

for future meals.

- Drink coffee or tea black.
- Use the hand guide to keep portion sizes reasonable: www.guardyourhealth.com.
- Harness the power of secret healthy ingredients. Make healthier versions of the foods you really enjoy eating.
- Roast instead of fry.
- Start observing meatless Mondays.
- Always pick unprocessed snacks.
- Have a glass of water between every alcoholic drink.
- Bring lunch to work at least once a week.
- Make smarter snacking choices (e.g., use apples instead of crackers).
- Eat your veggies first, then the rest of your plate.
- Use at least half whole-grain flour in baking recipes.
- Join a CSA (community-supported agriculture).
- Drink seltzer instead of soda.
- Eat savory proteins and veggies for breakfast instead of carbs and sweets.
- Use smaller plates.
- When cooking eggs, use the whites and less yolks.
- Eat as many colors as possible every day.
- Make smart ingredient swaps.
  - Use oat bran for flour.
  - Use mashed bananas for oil or butter.
  - Spaghetti squash instead of pasta.

- Citrus fruit instead of salt to flavor.

- Unsweetened applesauce in place of sugar.

- Plain Greek yogurt in place of sour cream.

- Avocado instead of mayo.

- Kale, spinach, or arugula instead of lettuce.

- Evaporated milk, not cream.

- Pureed fruit.

- Extra-lean ground beef.

- Light products.

- Two egg whites in place of a whole egg.

- Sneak seeds into everything.

- Have fresh fruit instead of a glass of juice.

- Make our meals at least one-half veggies.

The Mediterranean diet is one diet that is highly recommended.

How can you start doing this new way of eating, that is the fare along the Mediterranean Sea? It lowers the risk of heart disease, cancer, Alzheimer's, and diabetes. While eating this diet, you focus on eating plant-based nutrient-rich foods that work together to keep the body disease-free and healthy.

The Mediterranean diet starts with a foundation of fruits, vegetables, whole grains, beans, nuts, and seeds. Whole grains are the core of the diet. Each meal contains one to two servings of grains.

Fruits and vegetables are key components of this diet. Eight or more servings of fruits and veggies per day is known to decrease heart disease and stroke. Make it your goal to include two servings of veggies for lunch and dinner and one to two servings of fruits per meal.

Legumes provide a great source of protein in the diet.

Fish is eaten twice a week.

Very little poultry is consumed.

Use olive oil in place of butter and margarine.

Regular physical exercise is a must.

Drink red wine in moderation: one to two glasses of wine per day for men and one glass of wine per day for women.

Here are seven simple steps to start your own Mediterranean diet:

1. Add more veggies and make them your main dish.

2. Eat small portions of meat.

3. Include low-fat milk, yogurt, and cheese.

4. Eat fish twice a week.

5. Focus on a variety of healthy fats like olive oil, nuts, and avocados.

6. Use whole grains.

7. Swap desserts for fresh fruit.

This is a lot of information, but the biggest principle is to eat less and move more to lose weight.

What are your goals to become healthier? To lose x pounds (try for one pound a week, as that is a sustainable goal)? What habits will you incorporate this week? Put it in your daily planner.

Stand up for your own health.

You ARE UNSTOPPABLE!

These are your mindset-changing activities to keep your motivation going:

- ♦ Daily affirmations: You now have four audios from me and so many resources and YouTube to do these.
- ♦ Daily see yourself at the weight and health you want to be at.
- ♦ Do your daily planner and add food, exercise, and how you feel. This is to create the habit of journaling.
- ♦ Visit your vision board and add pictures of your ideal body if you have not done so.
- ♦ Go bless others as you change your life. HAVE FUN!

Nutrition Primer

You are what you eat. You are responsible for what you put into your body.

Proper nutrition consists of having enough energy intake to meet your body's demands. Adequate macronutrients (carbohydrates, protein, and fat) and micronutrients (vitamins and minerals) are essential; they allow the body to function as a powerful, magnetic you! Fluid intake is critical as well, so keep that water bottle handy.

The USDA has developed guidelines that reveal the nutritional needs of a healthy person. The carbohydrate intake for a person depends on the activity level of the person. A rough estimate is five grams of carbohydrates per kilogram of body weight (one kilogram is equal to 2.2 pounds). Carbohydrates get a bad rep in the keto diet and others. They are essential for energy production and keep the immune system functioning well.

Protein is the second macronutrient the body needs. The functions of protein are building tissue, making enzymes, and being an alternative energy source. Two types of protein exist: complete protein (which has all nine amino acids) and incomplete protein. Animal sources are complete proteins, with eggs being the gold standard. Animal proteins are also more protein dense. Many plant sources lack one or more of the essential amino acids. Soybeans, however, are a complete protein. For a person following a vegan diet to have all their protein needs met, they need to eat a variety of plants, grains, and legumes. The RDA for a normal person (sedentary) is 0.8 grams per kilogram of body weight. For a typical 130-pound female, this is 47 grams of protein per day. Typically, if you eat any meat at all, the RDA is met.

Fat is the third macronutrient. There are two essential fatty acids that must be obtained from the diet. Fat is a large energy reservoir and works really well to support long exercise activities. Fat is necessary for proper immune function and for protecting the organs through layers of padding around the organs. Fat should be less than 30 percent of the total energy intake. Of this intake, 10 percent should be saturated, 10 percent monounsaturated, and 10 percent polyunsaturated. In each gram of fat, there are 9.4 calories. Our 130-pound average female needs 60 grams of fat per day in her diet from all sources and the older we are, the more important protein is.

Here is a link from the USDA to calculate your daily requirements of macro and micronutrients: https://www.nal.usda.gov/fnic/dri-calculator/index.php.

DRI calculator results

Daily nutrient recommendations are based on the Dietary Reference Intakes (DRIs) by age and gender. Nutrient recommendations based on the DRIs are meant to be applied to generally healthy people of a specific age and gender set. Individual nutrient requirements may be higher or lower than the DRIs. Consult a healthcare professional to determine individual nutrient requirements for those with specific health or medical conditions. Learn more about the DRIs at https://www.nal.usda.gov/legacy/fnic/dri-nutrient-reports.

When looking at results, keep in mind the following:

- DRI amounts are set at levels to meet the nutrient requirements of almost all healthy people. Each reference value refers to the **average daily nutrient intake**. Some deviation around this average value is expected over several days. In fact, nutrient amounts derived from day-to-day intake may vary substantially without ill effect. Access the DRI reports for in-depth information on using the DRIs for planning and assessing dietary intake as well as obtaining detailed reports on each of the nutrients.

- Foods provide a variety of nutrients and other compounds that have healthful effects. Nutritional needs should be met primarily through eating a variety of foods as outlined in the *Dietary Guidelines for Americans 2015–2020*.

Additional resources include the following:

- ChooseMyPlate.gov
- FoodData Central
- USDA Food Surveys Research Group
- Nutrition.gov – this is a fun tool to use to see what your daily requirements are.

When you put in your data, a report is generated as shown here.

This table is only for a quick reference or until you print out your own data. It is a tad boring, yet it contains a wealth of information about your body's needs.

You entered:	
Sex	Female
Age	52 years
Height	5 ft. 7 in.
Weight	120 lbs.
Activity level	Very Active
Pregnancy/Lactation status	Not Pregnant or Lactating

This table contains the calculated results of your body mass index (BMI) and your estimated daily caloric needs. This table is ordered similarly to the previous one. Results:

Body Mass Index (BMI)	18.8

The table below contains your daily required macronutrients and the daily recommended intake of each macronutrient. Macronutrients:

Macronutrient	**Recommended Intake Per Day**
Carbohydrate	284 - 410 grams
Estimated Daily Caloric Needs	2,525 kcal/day
Total Fiber	21 grams
Protein	44 grams
Fat	56 - 98 grams
Saturated fatty acids	As low as possible while consuming a nutritionally adequate diet.

This table contains the calculated results of your body mass index (BMI) and your estimated daily caloric needs. This table is ordered similarly to the previous one. Results:

Body Mass Index (BMI)	18.8
Trans fatty acids	As low as possible while consuming a nutritionally adequate diet.
α-Linolenic Acid	1.1 grams
Linoleic Acid	11 grams
Dietary Cholesterol	As low as possible while consuming a nutritionally adequate diet.
Total Water	2.7 liters (about 11 cups)

This table contains the vitamins that you require daily, the recommended intake of each vitamin, and the highest amount of each vitamin that you can intake. Vitamins:

Vitamin	Recommended Intake Per Day	Tolerable UL Intake Per Day
Vitamin A	700 mcg	3,000 mcg
Vitamin C	75 mg	2,000 mg
Vitamin D	15 mcg	100 mcg
Vitamin B_6	1.5 mg	100 mg
Vitamin E	15 mg	1,000 mg
Vitamin K	90 mcg	0 mcg
Thiamin	1.1 mg	0 mg
Vitamin B_{12}	2.4 mcg	0 mcg
Riboflavin	1.1 mg	0 mg
Folate	400 mcg	1,000 mcg

This table contains the vitamins that you require daily, the recommended intake of each vitamin, and the highest amount of each vitamin that you can intake. Vitamins:

Vitamin	Recommended Intake Per Day	Tolerable UL Intake Per Day
Vitamin A	700 mcg	3,000 mcg
Vitamin C	75 mg	2,000 mg
Niacin	14 mg	35 mg
Choline	0.425 g	3.5 g
Pantothenic Acid	5 mg	0 mg
Biotin	30 mcg	0 mcg
Carotenoids	NA	ND

This table contains the minerals that you require daily, the recommended intake of each mineral, and the highest amount of each mineral that you can intake. They are classified by essential and non-essential minerals. Minerals (Elements):

Mineral	Recommended Intake Per Day	Tolerable UL Intake Per Day
Essential		
Calcium	1,200 mg	2,000 mg
Chloride	2 g	3.6 g
Chromium	20 mcg	0 mcg
Copper	900 mcg	10,000 mcg
Fluoride	3 mg	10 mg
Iodine	150 mcg	1,100 mcg
Iron	8 mg	45 mg
Magnesium	320 mg	350 mg
Manganese	1.8 mg	11 mg

This table contains the vitamins that you require daily, the recommended intake of each vitamin, and the highest amount of each vitamin that you can intake. Vitamins:

Vitamin	Recommended Intake Per Day	Tolerable UL Intake Per Day
Vitamin A	700 mcg	3,000 mcg
Vitamin C	75 mg	2,000 mg
Molybdenum	45 mcg	2,000 mcg
Phosphorus	0.7 g	4 g
Potassium	2,600 mg	0 mg
Selenium	55 mcg	400 mcg
Sodium	1,500 mg	0 mg
Zinc	8 mg	40 mg
Non-Essential		
Arsenic	NA	ND
Boron	0 mg	20 mg
Nickel	0 mg	1 mg
Silicon	NA	ND
Sulfate	NA	ND
Vanadium	0 mg	1.8 mg

These charts are provided merely as a resource. There are so many available. It was my desire to provide a reference if you had not seen them before or just needed a refresher. They are not fun, yet they are important to know how to fuel our wonderful bodies for the best performance.

Micronutrients are nutrients that the body needs in small quantities. I will include a link to a resource from the Linus Pauling

Institute describing each micronutrient and its function, source, and daily intake recommendation. The B vitamins are all easy to get from a modern American diet that is not restricted. The fat-soluble vitamins (A, D, E, and K) are available from the diet and should not be taken over the recommended levels, as they are stored in our fat reserves and can accumulate in the body. Vitamin C is available readily in the diet from bright fruits and veggies. The list of minerals the body needs is lengthy, but most are commonly found in a well-rounded diet.

The key is to maintain balance and not fall for nutritional quackery in a diet or in supplements.

Melvin Williams poses several excellent questions in evaluating a supplement or diet:

- Does the product/diet promise quick improvements?
- Does it contain some secret, special ingredient or formula?
- Does the advertisement rely mainly on anecdotal evidence or celebrity endorsements?
- Does it exaggerate the benefit?
- Does it use outdated research or a single study to support its claim, or is the research published in a peer-reviewed journal?
- Is it a recent discovery that no one else has made?
- Is the claim(s) too good to be true?

By putting any supplement or diet to this test, you will save yourself a lot of headaches and save money as well on products that don't work.

Weight management is achieving your ideal body weight, which is the weight at which your health risk is the lowest. This is a simple calculator to come up with your ideal body weight: https://www.calculator.net/ideal-weight-calculator.html. This site has a plethora of useful information. So, I encourage you to try the link and have fun playing with all the calculators offered.

The reason weight management is so important is that there are significant health risks to being overweight. These include cardiovascular disease, hypertension, type 2 diabetes, pulmonary disorders, sleep apnea, gout, cancer, arthritis, depression, and early mortality.

Obesity is caused by an imbalance between physical activity and food consumption, psychological and cultural factors, social psychology, food production and choices, physiology, thyroid gland malfunction, and genetic predisposition.

Sometimes people use these poor weight management strategies:

- Fad diets, which are effective short-term, not nutritionally balanced, too severe to maintain, and cause a decrease in metabolic rate.

- Diuretics increase urination, which only leads to dehydration and electrolyte imbalances, which can be harmful to your health.

- Stimulants to suppress the appetite.

- Massage, which is not effective for weight loss at all

- Surgery to wire the jar shut, gastric bypass, or liposuction.

None of these are safe or effective, yet they are misused daily by many, many people.

There are many effective guidelines for sound weight control. The first is to improve your diet. Have a balanced and sustainable diet. Do not lose more than one to two pounds a week so the body can adapt to each change slowly and well. Utilize portion control and eat nutrient-dense foods that fill you up. Finally, you must be honest with yourself about how much you are or are not consuming.

Changing your eating habits is key to effective weight management. Some tips are to not go shopping when you are hungry so you don't buy food that is not healthy for you, shop from a list and stick to it to save calories and dollars, eat slowly and wait twenty minutes for your brain to catch up with what you put in your stomach, buy and use smaller plates to give your brain the idea that you have a full plate, eat breakfast, and eat more often in smaller quantities to keep your blood sugar at a level of homeostasis. This is a great little tip that gives you a nice reward at the end of your meal. Have a signal that tells your brain and body that the meal is over. Perhaps a little piece of nice chocolate will be all you need.

By improving the level and quality of your exercise, you increase your caloric consumption and boost your metabolism. Exercise builds muscle, which increases your basic metabolic rate. Exercise helps relieve depression and anxiety. You must commit to it for the rest of your life and find activities that you enjoy and that you will do for the rest of your life.

Proper nutrition and weight management are key elements to living a more powerful and magnetic lifestyle. It takes time, determination, and commitment to yourself. The rewards far exceed the training process to eat properly and maintain your weight. You will look great and feel great too.

The following are some links of interest from government websites to give you materials to keep learning:

- www.cdc.gov/healthyweight/losing_weight/index.html
- www.webmd.com/diet/obesity/healthy-weight#1

♦   www.niddk.nih.gov/health-information/weight-management

MEDITERRANEAN DIET 101:
A MEAL PLAN AND BEGINNER'S GUIDE

The Mediterranean diet is based on the traditional foods that people used to eat in countries like Italy and Greece back in 1960. Researchers noted that these people were exceptionally healthy compared to Americans and had a low risk of many lifestyle diseases. Numerous studies have now shown that the Mediterranean diet can cause weight loss and help prevent heart attacks, strokes, type 2 diabetes, and premature death.

There is no one right way to follow the Mediterranean diet, as there are many countries around the Mediterranean Sea, and people in different areas may have eaten different foods. This article describes the dietary pattern typically prescribed in studies that suggest it's a healthy way of eating. Consider all of this as a general guideline, not something written in stone. The plan can be adjusted to your individual needs and preferences.

How to follow it

♦   Eat: vegetables, fruits, nuts, seeds, legumes, potatoes, whole grains, bread, herbs, spices, fish, seafood, and extra virgin olive oil

♦   Eat in moderation: poultry, eggs, cheese, and yogurt.

♦   Eat only rarely: red meat.

♦   Don't eat sugar-sweetened beverages, added sugars, processed meat, refined grains, refined oils, and other highly processed foods

Avoid these unhealthy foods

You should avoid these unhealthy foods and ingredients:

- Added sugar: soda, candies, ice cream, table sugar, and many others.
- Refined grains: white bread, pasta made with refined wheat, etc.
- Trans fats: found in margarine and various processed foods
- Refined oils: soybean oil, canola oil, cottonseed oil, and others
- Processed meat: processed sausages, hot dogs, etc.
- Highly processed foods: anything labeled 'low-fat' or 'diet' or which looks like it was made in a factory.

You must read food labels carefully if you want to avoid these unhealthy ingredients.

Foods to eat

Exactly which foods belong to the Mediterranean diet is controversial, partly because there is such variation between different countries. The diet examined by most studies is high in healthy plant foods and relatively low in animal foods.

However, eating fish and seafood is recommended at least twice a week.

The Mediterranean lifestyle also involves regular physical activity, sharing meals with other people, and enjoying life.

You should base your diet on these healthy, unprocessed Mediterranean foods:

- Vegetables: tomatoes, broccoli, kale, spinach, onions, cauliflower, carrots, Brussels sprouts, cucumbers, etc.

- Fruits: apples, bananas, oranges, pears, strawberries, grapes, dates, figs, melons, peaches, etc.

- Nuts and seeds: almonds, walnuts, macadamia nuts, hazelnuts, cashews, sunflower seeds, pumpkin seeds, etc.

- Legumes: beans, peas, lentils, pulses, peanuts, chickpeas, etc.

- Tubers: potatoes, sweet potatoes, turnips, yams, etc.

- Whole grains: Whole oats, brown rice, rye, barley, corn, buckwheat, whole wheat, and whole-grain bread and pasta

- Fish and seafood: salmon, sardines, trout, tuna, mackerel, shrimp, oysters, clams, crab, mussels, etc.

- Poultry: chicken, duck, turkey, etc.

- Eggs: chicken, quail, and duck eggs

- Dairy: cheese, yogurt, Greek yogurt, etc.

- Herbs and spices: garlic, basil, mint, rosemary, sage, nutmeg, cinnamon, pepper, etc.

- Healthy Fats: extra virgin olive oil, olives, avocados, and avocado oil

Whole, single-ingredient foods are the key to good health.

What to drink

Water should be your go-to beverage on a Mediterranean diet. This diet also includes moderate amounts of red wine—around one glass per day.

However, this is completely optional, and wine should be avoided by anyone with alcoholism or problems controlling their consumption.

Coffee and tea are also completely acceptable, but you should avoid sugar-sweetened beverages and fruit juices, which are very high in sugar.

A Mediterranean sample menu for one week

Below is a sample menu for one week on the Mediterranean diet. Feel free to adjust the portions and food choices based on your own needs and preferences:

Monday

- Breakfast: Greek yogurt with strawberries and oats
- Lunch: a whole-grain sandwich with vegetables
- Dinner: a tuna salad dressed in olive oil, a piece of fruit for dessert

Tuesday

- Breakfast: oatmeal with raisins
- Lunch: leftover tuna salad from the night before
- Dinner: salad with tomatoes, olives, and feta cheese

Wednesday

- Breakfast: omelet with veggies, tomatoes, and onions, a piece of fruit
- Lunch: a whole-grain sandwich with cheese and fresh vegetables
- Dinner: Mediterranean lasagna

Thursday

- Breakfast: yogurt with sliced fruits and nuts
- Lunch: leftover lasagna from the night before
- Dinner: broiled salmon served with brown rice and vegetables

Friday

- Breakfast: eggs and vegetables, fried in olive oil
- Lunch: Greek yogurt with strawberries, oats, and nuts
- Dinner: grilled lamb with salad and baked potato

Saturday

- Breakfast: oatmeal with raisins, nuts, and an apple
- Lunch: a whole-grain sandwich with vegetables
- Dinner: Mediterranean pizza made with whole wheat, topped with cheese, vegetables, and olives

Sunday

- Breakfast: omelet with veggies and olives
- Lunch: leftover pizza from the night before
- Dinner: grilled chicken with vegetables and potato, fruit for dessert

There is usually no need to count calories or track macronutrients (protein, fat, and carbs) on the Mediterranean diet.

For more ideas, check out this list of 21 healthy Mediterranean recipes.

Healthy Mediterranean Snacks

You don't need to eat more than 3 meals per day.

Snacks between meals:

- A handful of nuts
- A piece of fruit
- Carrots or baby carrots
- Some berries or grapes
- Leftovers from the night before
- Greek yogurt
- Apple slices with almond butter

A Simple Shopping List For The Diet

It is always a good idea to shop at the perimeter of the store. That's usually where the whole food is. Always try to choose the least processed option. Organic is best if affordable:

- Vegetables: carrots, onions, broccoli, spinach, kale, garlic, etc.
- Fruits: apples, bananas, oranges, grapes, etc.
- Berries: strawberries, blueberries, etc.
- Frozen veggies: choose mixes with healthy vegetables.
- Grains: whole-grain bread, whole-grain pasta, etc.
- Legumes: lentils, pulses, beans, etc.
- Nuts: almonds, walnuts, cashews, etc.
- Seeds: sunflower seeds, pumpkin seeds, etc.
- Condiments: sea salt, pepper, turmeric, cinnamon, etc.

- Fish: salmon, sardines, mackerel, trout

- Shrimp and shellfish

- Potatoes and sweet potatoes

- Cheese

- Greek yogurt

- Chicken

- Pastured or omega-3-enriched eggs.

- Extra virgin olive oil

It's best to clear all unhealthy temptations from your home, including sodas, ice cream, candy, pastries, white bread, crackers, and processed foods. If you only have healthy food in your home, you will eat healthy food.

THE BOTTOM LINE

Though there is not one defined Mediterranean diet, this way of eating is generally rich in healthy plant foods and relatively lower in animal foods, with a focus on fish and seafood.

You can find a whole world of information about the Mediterranean diet on the Internet, and many great books have been written about it.

Try googling 'Mediterranean recipes,' and you will find a ton of great tips for delicious meals.

At the end of the day, the Mediterranean diet is incredibly healthy and satisfying. You won't be disappointed.

The fruits of tomorrow are in the seeds of today. What you put in, you get out. Basic sowing and reaping principles. Remember to never compromise who you are now and who you will be for anyone.

Your journey is beautiful because you are. You are far more loved than you could ever imagine. Even if you feel like you are starting over time and time again, do it for you. One day, when you look back and observe your progress, you will understand why it has all happened as it has. You are worth pushing yourself because no one else is going to do it for you!

Eating properly does take a bit more time in food preparation and purchasing, but that can be a fun experience. Learning about new foods and new recipes can be fun to do, and you can always add in your family members. Since we can't all have a personal chef to do the buying, prepping, and preparation for us, we can just make it more fun. You can focus on lower costs one time, easier preparation another time, more protein-focused one week, less gluten another week, and the possibilities are endless.

What made me a big fan of the Mediterranean diet was spending a week with the Greeks. After this time, I have tried to have my own diet and my family's diet be centered around the Greed cuisine. As I think back on it, my mouth is watering from how delicious the cuisine is. To eat the fresh tomatoes raw or on a bed of freshly picked lettuce or kale topped with fresh mozzarella cheese. Drizzle olive oil over the top—and yummy, a salad has been created.

Good nutrition is crucial. Although time-consuming, the effort is worthwhile. I couldn't have made it through a single day at Cape Epic without paying close attention to what I put into my body. Without paying close attention to the fuel for my engine, I would not have been able to finish 8 days of intense racing/riding. Spending so much energy working up an appetite is exhausting. Eating becomes tedious, but you know you should persevere or risk not finishing. For my eight-hour daily ride, I needed to consume 50–60 grams of food, or roughly 10 energy bars. It becomes tiresome to do or transport.

But I had to reframe my thoughts and language to reflect the reality that I rely on food for energy. I need to replenish my energy stores because I am expending so many calories. So, keeping a cheerful heart and speaking encouraging thoughts, I concluded my work. It was important for me to keep myself and my coaches accountable so that we could finish the marathon. Because large races, and life more generally, are far more difficult without the right crew behind you. Anything is achievable with the right team on board. Good nutrition is crucial. Although time-consuming, the effort is worthwhile. I couldn't have made it through a single day at Cape Epic without paying close attention to what I put into my body. Without paying close attention to the fuel for my engine, I would not have been able to finish 8 days of intense racing/riding. Spending so much energy working up an appetite is exhausting. Eating becomes tedious, but you know you should persevere or risk not finishing. For my eight-hour daily ride, I needed to consume 50–60 grams of food, or roughly 10 energy bars. It becomes tiresome to do or transport. But I had to reframe my thoughts and language to reflect the reality that I rely on food for energy. I need to replenish my energy stores because I am expending so many calories. So, keeping a cheerful heart and speaking encouraging thoughts, I concluded my work. It was important for me to keep myself and my coaches accountable so that we could finish the marathon. Because large races, and life more generally, are far more difficult without the right crew behind you. Anything is achievable with the right team on board.

CHAPTER FIVE

The Support Staff

The start of each day at Cape Epic - The first bus will leave at 6:30, the second at 7:00, and the third and last at 7:30. Our concierge would wake us up and put us to bed with a kind reminder that we couldn't keep our teammates waiting. Breakfast is served between 5:30 and 7 a.m. on race days. Spend eight hours pedaling nonstop at the world's hardest race. Dinner begins at 6:30, and massages are offered before and after. Focus like a laser for the next week. Our support staff makes it feasible for riders to complete the Cape Epic. Johan and Alex were the most charming concierges. They made sure that each guest was comfortable. It was a pure delight to come back to such a cozy room after an exhausting day. It felt great to take a long, hot shower after working in the dirt all day.

That much food every day could be difficult to consume, and after a while it might all start to taste the same. If you want to finish a stage race of this magnitude, you need to take care of yourself, and that includes eating until you›re sick of eating. When training at this level of intensity, self-care, diet, and sleep become paramount. Without the help of our gracious hosts, we would have been in the same dire situation as the people living in the red tent city. Even so, with Johan and Alex›s assistance, daily preparation was a breeze. Johan arranged the best mechanics we›ve ever had worked on our bicycles. The massage therapists did a fantastic job of smoothing out all the kinks in our tired muscles. It was also part of a massage therapist›s job to simply listen, as sometimes that›s all you need to get through the day.

Thanks to excellent planning and teamwork, working hard was actually delightful. This exemplified the highest levels of selflessness on their behalf and compassion on ours. Sometimes, you need to open up your life to other people and accept their assistance. Our goal was to compete at the greatest level of our sport, and having a solid support structure helped us get there. How far would you go to assist yourself? How can you improve your chances of being surrounded by people who appreciate you for who you really are?

A mature person can absorb constructive criticism and is open to new ideas. Be cautious whenever your mind wanders to your future self.

What are we waiting for? Involvement in any form of physical activity, such as walking, swimming, cycling, jogging, skiing, yoga, stand-up paddleboarding, group programs at the Y, etc., can have numerous positive effects on one's health and well-being. Getting moving and treating it like a game is priority number one. A minimum of 150 minutes of exercise per week is suggested. When coupled with a balanced diet, this will not only help your heart, but it will also improve your mood, energy level, and sleep quality.

Simply moving forward will do the trick. The path to being your most confident, alluring self can be started at any time. The need to maintain a regular exercise routine to ensure continued health and vitality as we age cannot be overstated.

Let's get started with some pointers:

Discover your driving force. The question is, "Why?" Is it to lose weight as recommended by a doctor, to boost energy levels, to improve your appearance, or to improve how you feel about yourself? Put up some inspiring images on your vision board and fridge to keep you going strong. For whatever reason, make that your emphasis. After you've seen firsthand the positive effects of regular exercise on your mood and energy levels, maintaining an active lifestyle will naturally become part of your routine.

All that is required is to just move and keep moving. Any day is a great day to start, and this is a huge component of the powerful, magnetic you! The older you are, the more important it is for you to maintain your health through exercise to benefit every area of life.

Let's get moving with the following tips:

- Find your motivation. What is your why? Is it to trim down a bit, to follow the doctor's orders, to have more energy, to look better, or to feel better? Get some pictures to look at on your refrigerator and your vision board to keep your motivation going. Whatever the reason is, keep focused on it as a goal! Eventually, it will become a part of your lifestyle, and after noticing how good staying active makes you feel, it will be easier to do!

- Keep it regular and make it a routine.
  - Get an accountability partner.
  - Keep track of it in your daily planner.
  - Make the time.
  - Exercise at the same time every day so it becomes part of your routine.

- Find a convenient time and place to do the activities; make it a flexible habit.

- HAVE FUN! LAUGH! ENJOY FRIENDS! ENJOY NATURE! ENJOY LIFE!

◆ Start slowly. Focus initially on low-intensity exercises that leave you feeling good. Try yoga or a fitness class. Every other day, train a different set of muscles, allow recovery time, and listen to your body. Don't overdo it, as recovering from injury at our age takes a little longer.

Keep this trifecta in mind to work on:

◆ Flexibility

◆ Strength

◆ Endurance

Flexibility. Start with flexibility, which will enhance how you feel and halt the start of osteoarthritis or slow down any existing arthritis. Stretch for 10 to 15 minutes twice a day or do positive mobility twice a day. You will feel incredible.

This is a simple routine to do at home:

1. Hip openers through touching your toes.

2. Gently twist your upper body, with your lower body stationary.

3. Lunges.

4. Clasp your hands behind your back and hold to stretch out your shoulders and frontal body.

5. Reach high and bend your torso to the left or the right.

Breathe into the tightness and relax.

Push yourself but within moderation.

Foam rolling is also a great addition to home stretching. Foam rollers are easy to obtain and are somewhat small.

Strength. After 50, you lose muscle mass unless you throw some resistance training into your training plan. Do it one to two times a week. You can do it at home with free weights and squats or hit the gym. You will feel sore at the beginning, but that means it is working. To alleviate this soreness, you can add some more stretching. POSITIVE MOBILITY TO INCREASE strength, balance, and flexibility.

Endurance. Experiment with what suits you. Personally, I love all types of outside play, but you may like a specific class or CrossFit. Awesome. JUST DO IT! The goal is 150 minutes per week, like 30 minutes five times a week. Even better would be 300 minutes or five hours a week. You can garden, walk, play with the dog, hike, bike, Zumba, CrossFit, swim, etc. The takeaway? Move more with more intensity and sit less.

Make it fun! Track your success in your daily planner. Add it to your gratitude journal. Be kind to yourself and take your time with the exercise trifecta—flexibility, strength, and endurance. The goal is a happier and healthier you—a powerful, magnetic You!

These tips can help add movement at work; every little bit helps:

- Take the stairs even for a flight or two at the beginning.
- Walk to the furthest bathroom.
- When on the phone for a while, pace in a circle or march in place.
- On a long call, or if you need an energizing break, stand up

and do squats, desk push-ups, wall sits, lunges, calf raises, the tree pose, and the chair pose.

- Keep small hand weights or a resistance band at your desk for bicep curls, lateral raises, rows, or overhead presses.

- Form a walking club at lunch and raise money for charity.

- Walk to meetings and use a voice memo app to capture notes.

- Walk to eat at a local restaurant or walk during lunch.

- Explore a standing desk, treadmill desk, or desk riser.

- Take lots of walking and stretching breaks.

The benefits of this will be some big wins: a decreased risk of heart disease, stroke, type 2 diabetes, HBP, dementia, Alzheimer's, and cancer; improved cognition, including memory, attention, and processing speed; less weight gain, obesity, and related chronic health conditions; better bone health and balance, with less risk of injury from falls; decreased symptoms of depression and anxiety; a better quality of life and sense of well-being; and better sleep, including improvement in insomnia and sleep apnea.

That is a huge list of benefits for such a small investment. Where else can you get such a large Return on your investment? SO, LET'S GET MOVING!

EXERCISE AND SLEEP = A RESTFUL COMBO

Moderate aerobic exercise increases slow-wave sleep. This form of sleep is deep sleep, where the brain and body can rejuvenate. Exercise can stabilize the mood. It decompresses the mind. It causes the body to release endorphins. It increases the body's core temperature like a wonderful hot shower, and it decreases insomnia.

A primary point is that if sleep evades you, then you undermine your body. To exercise better, you must pay attention to what you eat, what you drink, and especially how you sleep. You must sleep.

Sleep allows your body to recover, conserve energy, and repair and rebuild the muscles you just exercised. We need growth hormones to help us build lean muscle, and it helps our body repair when we have torn ourselves up during a hard workout. Growth hormones are essential for athletic recovery, and the way we get it is by sleeping, specifically seven or so hours a night. Exercise helps get us there and keeps us sleeping.

Adenosine is a brain chemical that is released when you exercise. When it is released, you start feeling sleepy. The harder your work out, the more adenosine is released, and thus, you experience a greater drive to fall asleep.

When adenosine is produced after working out, it helps maintain your circadian rhythm. Morning exercise primes your body to sleep better at night. Working out before bed creates more efficient sleep. Moderate-intensity workouts before bed also help soothe pre-sleep anxiety. Low-intensity workouts like yoga are also helpful.

Exercise and sleep are your ultimate stress busters. Getting enough of both helps keep your stress at bay. Getting better sleep improves our workouts. It also gives you the motivation to stick to your workout plans.

Sleep deprivation causes you to fatigue quicker in your workouts. Sleep loss is linked to physiological responses like autonomic nervous system imbalances, which are like overtraining symptoms: sore muscles and increased risk of injuries.

If you have to select between sleep or a workout, choose sleep. If you are not getting seven to eight hours of sleep a night, do so and adjust your schedule to fit a workout in and sleep.

SEVEN STRATEGIES TO NAVIGATE INSOMNIA

- Physical. If you are physically struggling to keep your eyes open, then go to bed earlier. You can also use deep breath work and restorative yoga.

- Mental. Mental rest deprivation shows up as a lack of concentration. You can turn off your screens and ground yourself in meditation.

- Social. You are just drained. Take a night off and reconnect with yourself.

- Creative. This can be alleviated by going on a walk. You can also surround yourself with inspiration.

- Emotional. Emotional tiredness can be aided by offloading your feelings onto a willing listener. You may have to talk for a while to just let it go.

- Sensorial. Sensorial rest deprivation shows up as being chronically anxious. Put away your technology, catch up with a friend or a book, and just be alone.

- Spiritual. Spiritual deprivation can be recharged by seeking out a purpose and finding something to ground you.

So, exercise and sleep go hand in hand!

Let's add this to our daily planner: "Get seven to eight hours of sleep." Since we are focusing on exercise, let's focus on making it the best we can. I must work on this as well, so we're all in this together.

To conclude this chapter, I want to share 64 ways to do self-care in simple yet effective ways to help you become a more powerful, effective you! (The references I used for this list are *Sacred Rest:*

Recover Your Life, Renew Your Energy, Restore Your Sanity, and www. Living365fit.com.)

Your mental, emotional, and physical health all depend on your ability to practice self-compassion and self-care. A strong, magnetic you include self-care practices like working out and eating right. Brene Brown has accumulated a wealth of data demonstrating the importance of self-care, which includes embracing our human frailties without guilt or shame. To feel better, mindfulness experts recommend devoting just 10 minutes per day to acts of kindness toward oneself. Real self-care entails being sympathetic toward oneself as you acknowledge and accept your flaws and work to improve upon them. Self-compassion entails doing your best without being hard on yourself when you fall short of your ideals. When caring for oneself, strike a balance, not a perfect one.

I wanted to include these self-care practices as lovely reminders of acts of gratitude that we can do for ourselves. Please enjoy and observe:

- Spend time with a parent or mentor, someone who makes you feel protected and inspired.

- Volunteer to help a cause that means something to you.

- Listen to music from one of the happiest periods of your life.

- Practice a mindfulness exercise, even if it's just deep breathing.

- Light some candles and enjoy a nice glass of your favorite wine.

- Think of three positives associated with your current hardships.

- Take a hot shower for at least 10 minutes, then change into some soft, clean clothes.

- Do some creative writing. Imagine a fantasy scenario and lose yourself in it.

- Go to bed early and make sure you get at least a full eight hours of sleep.

- Make an appointment to see a therapist. Even just one session of unburdening yourself could make a difference.

- Say out loud, "Nothing lasts forever. This, too, shall pass."

- Visualize a beautiful, calm location and spend 10 minutes imagining you are there now.

- Keep your hands busy with a repetitive activity like knitting, sewing, or solving a puzzle.

- Write down 10 things in your life that inspire gratitude.

- Sketch something, whether it's an elaborate drawing or just a doodle of patterns that appeal to you.

- Go for a hike.

- Plan a day trip and take photographs of 10 things you see that inspire you.

- Look into local retreats where you can meet like-minded people and escape from society.

- Watch YouTube videos of cute animals.

- Hug someone you love for 12 to 15 seconds. Studies show that this boosts the immune system's function and prompts the release of calming hormones.

- Do some yoga. Even just five minutes of very basic positions can help you feel calmer and stronger.

- Go to a café, order your favorite delicious coffee, and read a book or magazine.

- Find any reminders of bad times and get rid of them. They are only adding negativity to your space.

- Slowly file, buff, and paint your nails, then massage soothing cream into your hands.

- Make a playlist of uplifting songs and know that you can tune in to it whenever things get rough.

- Let yourself cry if you need to. Holding it back tends to make people feel worse and not better.

- Challenge yourself to write down one hundred things you love about life. This is an excellent challenge, and it's easier than you might think.

- Just say no if someone is asking you to do something that feels too much.

- Recreate a favorite date or day out with your partner or a good friend.

- Take a full day and just take care of yourself.

- Eat a square of dark chocolate, which is proven to lower the levels of certain stress hormones.

- Skip your household chores for a full day.

- Watch several episodes of your favorite TV show back-to-back.

- Empty your wardrobe and donate old, ill-fitting, or unappealing clothes to charity.

- If you need to make a tricky decision, create a list of pros and cons and weigh the list to choose the best.

- Head to the gym and sweat out your stress with a serious workout.

- Head to a beautiful, quiet place and watch the sunset.

Bonus points if you can find one somewhere by the water.

- Dance to your favorite songs and really put your whole body into it!

- Watch a movie that is guaranteed to make you laugh.

- Go cycling or running in a beautiful place (you'll get the endorphins flowing and expose your mind to natural beauty).

- Get your favorite comfort food and savor it without any guilt. Just don't do it too often.

- Go for a drive with your music turned up loud. Sing along if you like.

- Switch off from the Internet for a full day.

- Go shopping and treat yourself to one little item that you don't really need but represents caring for yourself.

- Take a long, slow walk, listening to some of your favorite relaxing music on your headphones.

- Reset your brain and revitalize your energy stores by taking a 15- to 20-minute nap.

- Plan a weekend away, whether it's by yourself or with some people whose company you love.

- Make a cup of tea and just sip it in quiet stillness. Solitude is so regenerating.

- Cook a healthy meal that's packed with delicious fresh vegetables.

- Deliberately externalize your feelings of stress, sadness, or frustration in a journal entry.

- Interact with your pet or go to a place where you can touch some animals.

- Pick up the phone and call someone who understands you.

- Reorganize your workspace, getting rid of clutter. Research shows that this helps declutter your mind too.

- Smile at yourself in the mirror. You'll be surprised at how quickly the smile becomes genuine.

- Read a great book.

- Offer to walk someone's dog for them.

- Play a sport or sign up to learn a new one. It's good for your social life and great for pent-up frustration.

- Watch some crazy-long TV series in a marathon to escape.

- Book a massage, manicure, or facial—maybe all three.

- Plan a night out or a night in with your favorite people.

- If you are religious or spiritual, spend some time praying.

- Take a hot bath with Epsom salts.

- Sit by a river or ocean and watch the movement of the water.

- Paint something. It can be as abstract or realistic as you like!

The trifecta: exercise, sleep, and self-care

The fifth chapter focuses on exercise, sleep, and self-care. Each one is very important to our general well-being and a vital component to becoming a powerful, magnetic you!

This wonder drug of exercise is free and can cost a great deal, depending on your sport (drug) of choice. I spend thousands a year on cycling, yet it is my passion. I love it, and each aspect makes me so excited to keep doing it over and over year after year. Let's find something for you to do and be passionate about. It will be so much fun!

Exercise. Exercise increases your mood because the brain releases chemicals that boost your emotions and reduce stress. I love those endorphins that are better at pain relief and stress relief than any illegal drug. When your heart and lungs work together well, you have more energy for daily activities. Exercise promotes better sleep, adds a spark to your sex life, and helps maintain a healthy weight and body image. Exercise prevents several diseases like high blood pressure, heart disease, stroke, diabetes, arthritis, and depression.

Tips we will cover to motivate you and help you maintain your exercise regimen are the following:

+ Make it fun for you.

+ Mix it up.

+ Make it social. Have a party!

+ Make it a priority in time.

+ Make a commitment to do it.

The goal is to learn to love exercise and enjoy the benefits like reduced stress and better sleep.

Sleep. Sleep is beautiful and often elusive. The goal for adults is seven to nine hours a night. That seems like a lot to me. So, I will practice the following sleep habits too. Maybe I can go from five to six hours to six to seven hours or more:

+ Unwind before bedtime and chill with stretching, visualization, meditation, or breathing exercises. Completing items on your to-do list before going to bed can help calm your racing thoughts.

+ Develop a sleep routine—same time down and same time up every day.

+ Exercise regularly and avoid strenuous exercise within four hours of bedtime.

- Avoid caffeine and alcohol within a few hours of bedtime. The half-life of caffeine is four to six hours—meaning, it can take a full day to get rid of what you had in the morning. Alcohol is a temporary sedative, but once the alcohol is processed, it stimulates the brain, causing sleep problems later in the night.

- Limit late-night electronics usage, as it can be overstimulating. The glow from electronic devices can inhibit natural sleep cycles.

- Keep your room quiet and dark. Maybe you have to use earplugs, and maybe you have to use a sleep mask.

- Your bed is your sanctuary, and it should be associated only with sleep and relaxation. If you have insomnia, get up and do something else until you feel tired enough to go back to sleep.

- Sweet dreams to all.

Self-care. Learning to put oneself first is the point. It's incredibly common for us to prioritize everything and everyone else but ourselves. However, we should all learn to unwind and engage in self-care routines to lessen the negative effects of stress and anxiety. Stress, worry, burnout, fatigue, poor focus, a weakened immune system (which can lead to cancer), and a lack of self-confidence are just some of the issues that can be ameliorated by taking time for relaxation and self-care.

A stronger, more attractive you can be built on the solid foundation of regular exercise, sufficient rest, and self-care.

Here is a list of self-care affirmations you can use:

- I love, accept, and appreciate myself and others

unconditionally.

- I choose to be blissfully happy and healthy in mind, body, and spirit.
- I am strong, empowered, and capable of anything.
- Every day, in every way, I am learning to embrace my imperfections.
- I am adventurous, fearless, and fierce.
- I am free from expectations and criticism.
- I am worthy of abundance and prosperity.
- I am a beautiful and unique individual.
- I am enough just as I am right now and always.
- I recognize where I've been and celebrate the person I'm becoming.
- I choose to let go of negative self-chatter.
- I am smart, courageous, and self-confident.
- I am loved.
- I choose not to take things personally.
- I believe in myself and offer value to others.
- I choose to forgive myself and others and to let go of the past.
- I nurture my passions and creativity by doing things I love.
- I am gentle with myself and treat myself with kindness.
- Every day, in every way, I get to know my authentic self.
- My self-care is worth making time for.
- I take great care of and love my body, for it is a temple. And I treat it with respect.

- I take time to nourish my whole self.

- I am a priority in my own life.

- I have compassion for myself and my mistakes, and I have the same for others.

- I dream big and create my life with intention.

- I honor my intuition and use it as a guide.

- I have the courage to say no and set healthy boundaries.

- I allow myself to heal.

- I am grateful for who I am.

- I am patient with myself.

- I am worthy of all things wonderful.

- I am in perfect health.

- I release self-doubt, self-defeat, and self-sabotage.

- I choose to live in the moment and take things one day at a time.

- I am the hero in my own life story.

- I release the false security of being a people pleaser.

- I choose to let go of what I can't control.

- I accept myself regardless of my mistakes.

- I choose freedom over being a victim and release all past pain and emotional baggage.

- My light shines bright. I am free to be me now and always!

How exhausted do you feel right now? This section discusses how you might lessen that burden by surrounding yourself with a stellar support team. It would be fantastic if you could reduce the stress in your life and so conquer the burnout that has plagued the last couple of decades. Your body's defenses against persistent illness will be enhanced. Taking care of your diet, getting plenty of exercise, getting enough sleep, and otherwise treating yourself well will result in a revitalized appearance. Your youthful appearance and demeanor will draw attention.

We may make the most of our downtime by consciously slowing down to care for ourselves. We need periods of transition in order to recharge. We are constantly bombarded with new crises and have no time to recover. Perhaps we stop between major life events so that we don't forget about them since that's how our bodies work. Maintaining long-term viability requires meeting our basic physiological, psychological, emotional, and spiritual requirements. When even a minute's break would be appreciated, we rush through it and miss out on the nuances of life.

Taking those minute-long breathers is apparently something I am still learning. I'm still getting the hang of sleeping and resting effectively. After decades of nonstop effort and zero buffer space in my life, I am just now discovering the art of self-care. So, I think I'm still figuring out how to be my own best support crew and reveling in the magical moments along the journey, just like the rest of you.

CHAPTER SIX

Reflection

———————

One aspect of endurance sports on the bike, windsurfing, or on the snow that has always captured my interest is that you get to just pit yourself against what you chose to overcome and see how your preparation has prepared you. It is super fun doing it with others too. When you are caught in a blizzard, and some in your group are lost, there is no room for anything less than your best. Riding on the bike for long hours requires focus and staying in the present moment. There is no margin for error or not being focused on your task at hand, as you may crash downhill and break bones.

There are always choices to make from the preparation phase, selecting the right equipment, selecting the right crew, selecting the proper food, and choosing the right path in the race. The goal is to navigate to the finish and be able to inspire others to do the same. With all of these in proper alignment, the goals will be accomplished.

Crossroads – what path will you choose?

A major focus of this book has been to encourage you to create some new thinking about which direction you would like your life to take. Life is full of a myriad of choices. Making choices has consequences, likewise, not making choices has consequences. The older you are, the less chance there is to correct ill-timed or ill-thought-out choices.

When we see an obituary, we see a birth year, a dash, and a year of death.

Linda Ellis wrote a beautiful poem titled "The Dash."

> *I read of a man who stood to speak*
> *At the funeral of a friend*
> *He referred to the dates on the tombstone*
> *From the beginning...to the end*
>
> *He noted that first came the date of birth*
> *And spoke the following date with tears,*
> *But he said what mattered most of all*
> *Was the dash between those years*
>
> *For that dash represents all the time*
> *That they spent alive on earth.*
> *And now only those who loved them*
> *Know what that little line is worth*
>
> *For it matters not, how much we own,*
> *The cars...the house...the cash.*
> *What matters is how we live and love*
> *And how we spend our dash.*
>
> *So, think about this long and hard.*
> *Are there things you'd like to change?*
> *For you never know how much time is left*
> *That can still be rearranged.*

If we could just slow down enough
To consider what's true and real
And always try to understand
The way other people feel.

And be less quick to anger
And show appreciation more
And love the people in our lives
Like we've never loved before.

If we treat each other with respect
And more often wear a smile,
Remembering this special dash
Might only last a little while

So, when your eulogy is being read
With your life's actions to rehash...
Would you be proud of the things they say
About how you spent YOUR dash?
– Linda Ellis

The dash represents the time you have spent living on earth. We have focused on making your life new and exciting. Now you are living the legacy you will leave. This poem is such a wonderful, short reminder to LIVE LIFE TO THE FULLEST. Let's celebrate now! Live life now and make the most of every moment so that your dash represents a beautiful LIFE well lived in each moment.

"Nothing is impossible! Don't give up. Know who you are. Have a vision. Keep going." —Attila Korosi

Live Life

Life is crazy.
And totally unpredictable ...
It's going to push you over,
Kick you while you're down,
And hit you when you try to get back up.
Not everything can beat you.
Things are going to change you,
But you get to choose which ones you let change you.
Listen to your heart,
Follow your dreams,
And let no one tell you what you're capable of.
Push the limits,
Bend the rules,
And enjoy every minute of it.
Laugh at everything.
Live for as long as you can.
Love all,
But trust none.
Believe in yourself,
And never lose faith in others.
Settle for nothing but only the best,
And give 110% in everything you do.
Take risks,
Live on the edge,
Yet stay safe,
And cherish every moment of it.
Life is a gift.
Appreciate all the rewards,
And jump on every opportunity.
Not everyone's going to love you,
But who needs them anyway?

Challenge everything,
And fight for what you believe.
Back down to nothing,
But give in to the little things in life,
After all, that is what makes you.
Forget the unnecessary,
But remember everything.
Bring it with you everywhere you go.
Learn something new,
And appreciate criticism.
Hate nothing,
But dislike what you want.
Never forget where you came from,
And always remember where you are going.
Live life to its fullest,
And have a reason for everything,
Even if it's totally insane.
Find your purpose in life,
And live it
(Family Friend Poems 2008)

How much longer we have to live is anyone's guess. Would you be pleased with the things your "friends" say about the way you lived your life when your eulogy is read, and your deeds are left for others to ponder? What actions can we take today to begin building a legacy for future generations? Make the most of each present moment.

What we do today will leave a legacy in the future.

The fortresses of tomorrow are built from the foundations we lay now.

For your legacy to endure, you must make the difficult choice to stop doing the things and thinking the way that water down your influence. Put the good stuff in, and get rid of the bad. To leave a lasting mark, you must begin now. The only way to alter the course of history is to take action in the here and now and keep going in the desired direction. You may find helpful advice on any topic by searching Google. Constantly seek knowledge and improvement. Atrophy sets in if we don't actively pursue development.

YOU CANNOT GROW UNLESS YOU ARE WILLING TO CHANGE. So, here are the first 10 tips:

- Be joyful and serve in ways that bring you joy.

- Angry, unhappy people leave sad legacies.

- Monitor your impact on others. When you make the biggest difference, do more of that!

- Develop and maximize your unique talents, strengths, and skills. Know yourself and bring yourself to all that you do.

- Do what matters now.

- Seize small opportunities; big things follow. Do it now and make a difference.

- Start with those closest to you and the ones you spend the most time with.

- Bring your best self to work and family. Everyone has at least two selves. Bring out the best one.

- Think of service to others, not success.

- Elevate the needs of others over your own.

"No one is useless in this world who lightens the burdens of another." —Charles Dickens

Suggestions from Ophrah on being the best You!

- When you are excellent, you will be remembered.

- Michael Jordan played basketball against himself, and he continued to raise the standards in every practice. His goal? Excellence. Is he remembered? Yes!

- Master your craft. Become fantastic at what you do. Stop comparing yourself to others.

- Provide service. When you serve using your gifts and talents, significance will follow.

- Take responsibility for your life to have the power to move forward.

- Solve problems. Your greatest legacy is those whose lives you touch. Pick a problem and solve it.

- Always do the right thing. Be excellent, and people will notice.

- Listen to the whispers in your life.

- Become the best version of yourself!

- Surround yourself with successful people.

- Be around people who want you to be the best you than you can be.

- Fill yourself to the fullest so your cup will runneth over.

- Giving gallon-sized offerings to pint-size people doesn't work.

- FIND YOUR TRUE PASSION AND FOLLOW THAT.

HAVE FUN! Use your gifts to illuminate the world around you! Be a powerful, magnetic you!

When we approach the midcentury chronologically, the act of leaving a legacy comes up in conversation. For most of us, we will leave a more modest legacy that doesn't change the world but does leave a lasting footprint that will be remembered by those whose lives we touch.

Some additional thoughts on how to leave a great legacy now and in the future follow:

- Support the people and causes that are important to you!
- Keep in touch with friends and give your life away.
- Reflect and decide what is most important in your life.
  - Did you grow and transform your life?
  - Did you make the changes you needed?
  - Did you find your truth?
  - Did you inspire others?
- Touching lives and exemplifying a truthful path is vital to living a powerful and magnetic life. A life lived with purpose is one that will allow your legacy to live on.
- Share your blessings with others.
  - Think of all the blessings you have now and be mindful of sharing with others the richness you have.
  - Give your abundance to others. A smile is a blessing of acknowledgment.
- Be a mentor to others. You have some significant truth to impart to others that will guide less-experienced people in your life. Being in such a rich relationship involves personal development and support.
- Pursue your passions because they are infectious.

Your PASSIONS are your legacy!

One of the key concepts of this course is to find and pursue your passion, as it allows you to see your destiny clearly. For life to be fun and amazing, you must pursue your passions to the fullest. It is contagious. Pursue your passions and keep looking for new adventures.

Leaving a legacy is such an important part of your life's work. A legacy develops from a life that is dedicated to self-reflection and purpose. What will be revealed and what will endure is a truthful and value-driven body of living.

In concluding this chapter, I want to leave with you quotes about being remembered for you to embrace. Turn them into your own affirmations as well. This course is only the beginning of a well-lived and the transformation we are all engaged in.

Tell others about your successes and this book, and let's keep going and living our dreams!

Quotes regarding Leaving a legacy and living a life Worth living Now:

The following quotes remind me of reasons to navigate the path of life toward the highest and best destiny for myself. Quotes are valuable to me as they say so much in just a few words. One of the most important people in my life says a few words but when he does, you know that each one is important. That is what a quote is to me. They are markers of focusing on the important things. They are like small packages of intensity and power. They are a gift I would like to leave you with as you navigate your destiny to becoming the best version of yourself possible.

"Nothing in life is to be feared, it is only to be understood. Now is the time to understand more, so that we may fear less." —Marie Curie

"Life's most persistent and urgent question is 'What are you doing for others?'" —Martin Luther King

"Life is a series of natural and spontaneous changes. Don't resist them—that only creates sorrow. Let reality be reality. Let things flow naturally forward in whatever way they like." —Lao Tzu

Vision without action is a daydream. Action without vision is a nightmare. —Japanese Proverb

"You have enemies? Good. That means you've stood up for something sometime in your life." —Winston Churchill

"Perspective is the biggest thing in life. We are built to do wonders. Have a clear vision and have the courage to follow your vision." —Attila Korosi

"Nothing is impossible! Don't give up. Know who you are. Have a vision. Keep going." —Attila Korosi

"Imagination is everything! It's the preview to everything coming in life." —Albert Einstein

"Our truest life is when we are in dreams awake." — Henry David Thoreau

"Only a life lived for others is a life worthwhile." —Albert Einstein

"Life must be lived as play." —Plato

"Execute every act of thy life as though it were thy last." —Marcus Aurelius

"Sometimes life hits you in the head with a brick. Don't lose faith." —Steve Jobs

"Our life is what our thoughts make it." —Marcus Aurelius

"Beware the barrenness of a busy life." —Socrates

"Life is a fight. It's a good fight of faith." —Joel Osteen

"What we think determines what happens to us, so if we want to change our lives, we need to stretch our minds." —Wayne Dyer

"There are two primary choices in Life: to accept conditions as they exist or accept the responsibility for changing them." —Denis Waitley

"Change the changeable, accept the unchangeable, and remove yourself from the unacceptable." —Denis Waitley

"Don't dwell on what went wrong. Instead focus on what to do next. Spend your energies on moving forward toward finding the answer." —Denis Waitley

"Personal development is the belief that you are worth the effort, time and energy needed to develop yourself." —Denis Waitley

"When you visualize, then you materialize." —Denis Waitley

"Chase your passion, not your pension." —Denis Waitley

"Your habits will determine your quality of life." —Denis Waitley

"Get excited and enthusiastic about your own dream. This excitement is like a forest fire—you can smell it, taste it, and see it from a mile away." —Denis Waitley

Here's some homework for you:

- Do your affirmations daily.
- Use your personal organizer daily to journal your progress and make celebrations when you achieve goals.
- Meditate on your confidence board.

Here is a list of positive declarations:

- I am successful in whatever I do.
- I plan my work and work on my plan.
- I focus on what is truly essential.
- I will make the most of new opportunities.
- Good flows to me, and good flows from me.
- I feel wonderful and alive.
- I feel the joy of abundance.
- I speak with confidence and calm assurance.
- The universe provides for my every want and need.
- I am healthy and happy.
- I have a lot of energy.
- I radiate happiness.
- Everything is getting better every day.
- My mind is calm.

- I am always on the path to success and victory.
- I find peace and joy in all aspects of my life.
- I have value, and I matter.
- I am a success in all that I do.
- I am happy.
- I feel joy, love, and abundance.
- I am one with my inner child.
- I am amazing.
- I can do anything.
- I am prepared to succeed.
- Positivity is a choice.
- I am fabulous, funny, and giving.
- I am outstanding.
- I am unique and special, and most importantly, I am me.
- I am financially free.
- I am perfect exactly as I am.
- I make positive, healthy choices.
- I am in control of my reactions.
- I find all solutions within me.
- All is well in my life.
- I organize my priorities with clarity.
- I forgive myself.
- I am forgiven.
- I will always be there for myself.
- I enjoy the variety of life.

- I take good care of myself.
- I am patient with myself.
- I let go of my past.
- I am evolving eternally.
- I know I can always upgrade.
- There is a gift for me in everything that I experience.
- I follow my inner guidance.
- I appreciate my physical body.
- I treat my body well.
- I take it easy.
- I make room for fun and playfulness.
- I appreciate intimacy.
- I am very good at letting go.
- I am grateful for my life.
- I love being myself.
- Time is on my side.
- I surrender to love.
- I invite bliss.
- I learn from my past.
- I am good at walking the talk.
- I enjoy being taken good care of by the universe.
- I create my reality on a continuous basis.
- My body is healthy.
- I am superior to negative thoughts and low actions.
- I forgive those who have harmed me in my past and

peacefully detach from them.

- I possess the qualities needed to be extremely successful.
- My business is growing, expanding, and thriving.
- My ability to conquer my challenges is limitless.
- My potential to succeed is infinite.
- I am courageous, and I stand up for myself.
- My thoughts are filled with positivity, and my life is plentiful and prosperous.
- I am blessed with an incredible family and wonderful friends.
- I am a powerhouse.
- My future is an ideal projection of what I envision now.
- I radiate beauty, charm, and grace.
- I am healthy.
- I wake up today with strength in my heart and clarity in my mind.
- My fears of tomorrow are simply melting away.
- My life is just beginning.
- I always have everything I need to be happy.
- I live a positive life and only attract the best in my life.
- I am peacefully allowing my life to unfold.
- Today and every day, I choose to be happy.
- I am fun and energetic, and people love me for it.
- My life overflows with happiness and love.
- Today is rich with opportunities, and I open my heart to receive them.

- I am thankful that I get to live another day.
- I see the world with beauty and color.
- I deserve whatever good comes my way today.
- I believe in myself.
- I radiate confidence, certainty, and optimism.
- I courageously open and move through every door of opportunity.
- I am in charge of my life.
- I have the power to live my dreams.
- I stand up for what I believe.
- I act with courage and confidence.
- I love myself more every day.

Here are some gratitude declarations for deep happiness from Jennifer Healey:

- I am learning to be grateful for what I have while being excited for what has yet to come.
- I am eternally grateful for the love I can give and for the love I have yet to receive.
- Whatever has happened, and whatever does happen, I'm certain that I can be grateful again.
- I am grateful for the helpful guides that sometimes appear in disguise to usher me back to love.
- I am grateful now, and that is keeping the door open for more blessings.
- Even devastation is an opportunity for transformation, and my gratitude evolves as I do.
- I welcome all of the ways the universe wants to bless me.

- If I approach this situation/experience/person with appreciation, I will be held in the arms of abundance.

- Whatever I see, I trust that the universe is supporting my highest good. I choose to see this season of my life, then, through the eyes of appreciation as best as I can.

- My thanksgiving is perpetual; it survives every obstacle because I am willing to keep it alive.

- The feeling of gratefulness expands my perspective and opens me up to new ways of living happily in this world; it's as if the whole universe is in my heart.

- I'm willing to see beauty where others see nothing; I can look beyond a rock and uncover the diamond. For the rocks and the diamonds, I am thankful because life is a rich experience that includes *everything*.

- The more you pay attention to what's already working in your life, the better it gets.

- My thanksgiving extends far beyond my thoughts; I bring a grateful spirit to each step and action I take.

- I choose to be thankful for the light of this new morning and for renewed energy and strength to be who I know I can be.

- I shine the light of appreciation on an otherwise dark situation; there is no darkness that can escape that light for long.

- I accept my burdens, and I accept my blessings, and so I transform my burdens into my blessings.

- I partner with peace today, and I do this through the power of keeping a grateful heart.

- I fully accept the joy that wants to surface in my life, and I accept it now in gratitude. Give thanks for your ability to give anything in life, even if all you can give is a 'thank you.'

♦ I choose to see peace instead. I am willing to trust that my life is exactly as it's meant to be. I can relax a little and be thankful for what I have now.

♦ In truth, my gratitude is an absolute magnet for the manifestation of all that I want.

"There is a calmness to a life lived in gratitude, a quiet joy." — Ralph H. Blum

STRATEGIES TO BUILD ON TO CREATE YOUR LEGACY

Do YOU have the courage to live a more powerful, magnetic life? Sure, you do with your own strength and the help of others dedicated to the same goals.

Let's do a self-assessment of your life right now. Get your journal out, and let's write down what rocks are in your way to being the person you want to be. Then for each one of your pieces of granite, do the following:

1. Name and claim that metamorphic piece of granite (e.g., "I do not think I am talented at speaking—a huge boulder when you are going to do podcasts!").

2. Analyze all the facets of that boulder (e.g., "I don't think I have an amazing voice. Will people be interested in what I have to say? How do I master technology?").

3. Confront each facet to get unstuck (e.g., "Everyone thinks their voice sounds weird. I won't know if they like it or not until we go live. To master technology, I can ask friends, use Google, and just start playing around.").

4. Decide where you are going and stick with your plan. Make it a part of your daily to-do list.

5. To review, to get out of a rut, and begin transforming your mind, you must embrace your current situation and analyze it. Then it will be easier to just get on with making the improvements you want. Decide what kind of life you want to live, make a plan, and stick with it.

Is this easy? No, but if you don't do something NOW, where will you be in a year or in five years? Stuck or living the life you were created to live?

Fear is your friend!

Embrace it and harness the energy in it. Fear and pain are great assets, for without each, we are less motivated to grow and change. My son so wanted to make it to the state level in cross-country running. He had made it a goal, yet injuries plagued him for a year. And he went into the season out of shape. Often, the pain of change made him want to quit, yet he kept putting one foot in front of the other. In all seasons, there were highs and lows. He never thought his time was fast enough.

The race day came, and he was excited and scared. And he had a couple of doubts. I would not entertain those. I looked at his fear, analyzed it, and took action to control what we could: gaining muscles to run, proper nutrition and clothing, and doing proper warm-ups. The execution of his goal had to come from within. He dialed in, focused, and did exactly what he needed to do. HE MADE IT, and I KNOW you can achieve all the dreams in your own heart.

The emotions you feel push you to learn new skills. As I write about the experience with my son, my own emotions get fired up, and I feel the emotions of the preparation and the race and the ecstasy of making it to the state level. Seeing that young man beam was so exhilarating. I can still feel all the anticipation and the thrill of victory. To get unstuck, you must feel what you want so badly. You must feel how you want to look and what it will be like to accomplish your dream. Perhaps it is weight loss. Go buy a couple of outfits in the size you want to achieve. Feel the fabric and how lovely you will look wearing it. Notice the attention you get as people gaze upon your empowered body and admire your willpower to GET OUT OF YOUR RUT. Your example inspires them to do more.

Give yourself the grace to change and grow. Watching a baby learn to walk is such a lesson in grace and growth. They don't worry that they'll fall or plop onto their backsides. They get up and try again. They repeat this hundreds of times until they get it and soon are running. At each milestone, they smile and grin from ear to ear. They don't get discouraged. They get up and try again. Go and do likewise in your own life.

Leave any anger, bitterness, or pain toward anyone. Let it go. The Ho'oponopono prayer is such a simple yet profound forgiveness prayer. Pray it with emotion and let each person go, including YOU! Do it over and over for each person or even yourself.

> *Please forgive me.*
> *I'm so sorry.*
> *I love you.*
> *Thank you!*

There are days I say this prayer at least a hundred times. Forgiveness releases guilt and then brings you freedom.

Here is some mindset-changing work for you to do:

- Do the following self-assessment of your boulders in your journal.
  - Name and claim them.
  - Analyze all the facets of the boulder(s).
  - Confront each facet of that boulder(s) to get unstuck.
  - Decide where you are going and stick with your plan.
- Memorize and use the Ho'oponopono prayer daily.
  - I am sorry.
  - Please forgive me.
  - I love you.
  - Thank you!
  - Work on character development through intention and repetition using the above affirmations. These are in the audio of affirmations for this module.
  - Create a vision board and dream big. This is a lot of effort, but it will be life changing. I can't wait to hear about it in the Q and A section!

WHATEVER YOU ARE THINKING ... THINK BIGGER!

It's difficult to leave a lasting impression in the present. It's difficult to know your life's mission and to actually live it. Both can have an impact in the present and the long run.

Who you are gives you a sense of direction. No one can love you any more than you already are loved. What you do is not as important as who you are.

You have complete agency over how you use your time, money,

and talents. You have the option to start giving your full attention and effort to whatever you do. It is your responsibility to convince yourself that your actions have value and significance. It is up to you to decide how you want to spend your time in order to achieve your goals and fulfill your purpose in life.

We're no longer on the right track. Our absence is not a cover for anything. Instead, we've decided to do what we can with our abilities to spread more beauty, goodness, and love in the world.

A lack of direction in life is an excellent justification for doing nothing. Because YOU can, act on a big scale.

Make a decision and then GO FOR IT! Get serious about something you've decided to focus on. Set a timer and stick to it. Make it meaningful such that it encourages and inspires you to continue developing and changing. Instead, how would you like to conceive of and articulate your mission? Put the thoughts about your life's meaning and purpose into your head.

Keep in mind that a blazing sense of purpose necessitates a great deal of effort. Someone who is confident in their life's mission and purpose will be awed by the journey ahead and be present for every moment. You are just where you belong, performing the duties to which you have been assigned. The world is lucky to have YOU in it. Life, love, and significance just seep out of you.

When we know why we're here, what we leave behind follows naturally.

HOW TO LEAVE A LASTING LEGACY:

- Appreciate your existence, for it is a precious gift. Our lifestyle is entirely self-determined. Setting lofty objectives that make the most of the little time we have is an indication that we value our lives. Life is a precious gift that should be treasured and honored.

- Have a positive attitude. Enjoy the journey that is your life. Relationships are like fertile soil; when you bring joy and enthusiasm to them, they bloom. To live a rich and fulfilling life, enthusiasm is essential.

- Live a life of Gratitude and be thankful. Think of things from a perspective of plenty. Consider the positive aspects of your situation. How you feel about things shapes your outlook on life. The way other people treat you will mirror your attitude. Keeping a positive outlook will bring you luck and happiness.

- Achieve self-acceptance. You are truly unique. Richness increases as one learns to accept oneself more fully. If you don't like something about yourself, change it. No one else possesses the same combination of skills as you, and no one else can write the book that only you can.

- Moral fiber. Truth is the bedrock upon which trust in interpersonal interactions rests. You'll have more confidence in yourself, and others will respect you more if you always tell the truth. When someone acts in accordance with their deepest values, others respond positively to them. As Stephen Covey advises, "start with the end in mind" and direct your efforts toward achieving your ultimate goals. When charisma disappears, all that's left is character.

- Respect people always. When you treat others with dignity, you boost your own sense of worth. Recognize and value the integrity and beliefs of others. The only way to leave a legacy that lasts is to show others how much you care about them. Anyone who has achieved great success has felt the same doubts and apprehensions that the rest of us experience. What set them apart was that they actively confronted their concerns and, more crucially, that they believed in themselves when no one else did. Success is owed to all of us, and it is within the reach of any of us.

- Do something that truly fulfills you. One of the most important choices we can make is to do job that we are truly passionate about, as it will consume a significant portion of our lives. Since our time on Earth is finite, it's important to find fulfilling job while we're here. When you commit yourself fully to a single cause, you are truly living your legacy. If you want to leave a legacy, start living it today.

The core message of this book is to make the most of each day and keep pushing forward until you achieve your goals. No one has made it there yet. All of us keep plugging away at it. The more optimistic resources we have at our disposal, the faster and more easily we may achieve our life goals. Maintain the excellent progress you've made toward an ever-greater quality of life.

EPILOGUE

As you reach the end of this book, I hope you'll recognize how much like a race the obstacles you face in real life may be. The same concepts will help you whether you're dealing with health concerns, contemplating a career change, or biking across Africa. You'll have to convince yourself that it's possible to make that progress. Creating a confidence board and making public announcements of your goals can be helpful in this regard. To get from A to B, you'll need to take care of your body. You can't fulfill your purpose without proper nourishment, rest, self-care, and physical activity. Recalling the moment, I crossed the finish line of the final race of the Cape Epic: Even as I tried to wrap my head around what I had just accomplished, I was aware of the effort it had taken to get me to this point. I started to cry from overwhelming thankfulness. I pray that your own personal epiphany will lead to similarly healthy new beginnings.

My son just competed in a track relay race with three other male competitors. As the second member of the quartet, it was his responsibility to provide a smooth handoff to the final member. It was imperative that there be no lag time between handoffs. As you progress toward your breakthrough, you will encounter similar feelings. There needs to be one last push as we all finish our metamorphoses, just like in an athletic competition. Let's finish strong, inspire one another, and help others along the path to greatness. We are like the horses in the Preakness in the home stretch; we are giving it our best. I now give you the opportunity to take the next step toward your personal breakthrough!

You have worth and value in this world. I wish I could spend some time with each of you, hearing about your life and what you've done to make the world a better place. This book was written to serve as a source of inspiration for you as you move forward into the next stage of your life. Each and every one of you are incredible, and I'm here to show my love and support. Plan for your goals with the knowledge that doing so will determine your fate. Use language and thought patterns that will lead you to your goal. If they aren't, then let's figure out how to move them. It doesn't take long to adopt a new perspective. Modifying your routine in even the smallest ways can have a profound impact over time. You'll have the stamina to push yourself to a new healthy frontier if you follow a regimen of eating well, getting enough sleep, and exercising. Create a strong team behind your goals and aspirations to help you get there. You'll feel a surge of positive energy as you make the decision that will set you on the course to living your best life, both now and in the future. For the sake of your communities and the world at large, I have no doubt that everyone of you will leave a remarkable and distinctive legacy. Helping you reach a new, healthier horizon together, both now and in the future.

ABOUT THE AUTHOR

Kathy Judson has always been like this. This book is the result of many years of simply doing the work. She feels blessed to have spent her childhood on a farm, where she could find peace in the open air and the sight of towering mountains. Through these experiences, she developed a deep respect for toil and the natural world that will last a lifetime. She first competed in cross country and track at the Division 1 level before turning to triathlon as a professional sport and ultimately finding her true calling in cycling. She has raced as a semi-pro cyclist at the national and international levels for over 35 years. She values her two amazing sons, both of whom are on a mission to improve the world, above all else. Apples don't get far from the tree, as the saying goes. Kathy already had a Ph.D. in pharmacy and a B.S. in human nutrition, so she decided to expand her education with a Master's in counseling. Since she nearly died of anorexia when she was 17, she has made it her mission to live a full life. Nope, not there yet, but always looking forward to the next peak.

Kathy is either on the peak of a mountain competing in trail races or on social media. You may reach her for epic retreats, coaching, public speaking, and media appearances.

www.ingramcontent.com/pod-product-compliance
Lightning Source LLC
Chambersburg PA
CBHW051536120626
46551CB00012B/1248